SHADOWED BY DEEP TIME

PAUL R. PINET

authorHOUSE

AuthorHouse™
1663 Liberty Drive
Bloomington, IN 47403
www.authorhouse.com
Phone: 1 (800) 839-8640

© 2017 Paul R. Pinet. All rights reserved.

No part of this book may be reproduced, stored in a retrieval system, or transmitted by any means without the written permission of the author.

Published by AuthorHouse 02/24/2018

ISBN: 978-1-5462-1837-1 (sc)
ISBN: 978-1-5462-1835-7 (hc)
ISBN: 978-1-5462-1836-4 (e)

Library of Congress Control Number: 2017917899

Print information available on the last page.

Any people depicted in stock imagery provided by Thinkstock are models, and such images are being used for illustrative purposes only. Certain stock imagery © Thinkstock.

This book is printed on acid-free paper.

Because of the dynamic nature of the Internet, any web addresses or links contained in this book may have changed since publication and may no longer be valid. The views expressed in this work are solely those of the author and do not necessarily reflect the views of the publisher, and the publisher hereby disclaims any responsibility for them.

CONTENTS

PART I: Textures of Deep Time

Philosophy Of Mountains 3
Unsparing Truth 8
Creation Story 16
Desert Dreamscape 22
Vitality Of Stone 29
Catastrophism 38

PART II: The Nature of Deep Time

Deep Time's Stonework 57
Deep Time's Transformations 69

PART III: Reverberations of Deep Time

Mountains And The Mind 77
What Am I? 82
Of Dying And Becoming 91
The Tree Of Life 100
Edge Effects 104
The Randomness Of True Harmony 110
Memory 122
A Natural History Of The Soul 134

To Marita, my heartfelt wife and best ever life companion.

PROLOGUE

Trained as a geologist and educated as a mountaineer, I've spent my life pondering the vagaries of time, particularly the deep-rooted variety that oversees the wear and tear of landscapes. Earth has an expansive antiquity that is measured out in billions of years. Within the sharp cliffs of ridgelines and the broken boulders of ravines are dark spaces suffused with the life-blood of deep time. Though ignored, the abstruse, temporal materialization of Earth overshadows the clock hours that control all aspects of our modern lives. As the poet Joseph Powell reminds us, "Our lives shrink to incandescent flames that blink on the surface of the lake."

The deep-time account of all existence – Earth's skin, which is vibrantly alive in the whispered heartbeats of outcrops, glaciers, and mountains – is stored quietly in the DNA scripture of all living beings, including the animal *Homo sapiens*. My life-long quest has been to uncover how the intricacies of Earth's deep past emerged and why this geologic, evolutionary history matters greatly to humans alive today.

My essays emphasize the deep push-and-pull of long-ago memories that have largely vanished from our present-day mindset. The splendor of our shadowed lives is what this book celebrates, an epic state of being, where, according to Jack Turner, "time is less dense, less filled with information; space is close; smell and hearing and touch reassert themselves." My hope is that this book will embolden readers to search for age-worn shadows and absorb the glow of Earth's deep time.

PART I
Textures of Deep Time

PHILOSOPHY OF MOUNTAINS

"For two and a half years, my only view was an old fence and a mountain of white rock. There was no uncertainty there, not even close. It was a concrete mountain, bare, no vegetation, and a cold wind blew off it during the winter. You understand? A wind that shook the fence with a sound I have in my head and can't blot out. The sound of a frozen, unyielding landscape…"

Arturo Perez-Reverte, 2009, *The Painter of Battles*

The most shameless displays of naked rock occur on the haunches of mountains. In outright defiance of gravity, these stony rumps are squeezed tightly and lifted skyward by colliding continents, raising crustal 'tsunamis' with crest lines that crisscross Earth. Fearing these stone waves, we baptize them with names – the Himalayas, the Alps, the Andes, the Rockies. These upsweeps of bruised stone are wild places that excite the two-dimensional drabness of our maps and the flatness of our imagination.

Appearances, however, deceive. Despite their rock-hard shoulders, mountains are ephemeral when viewed against the slow creep of deep time. Under the incessant blur of wind, rain, and ice, rock slabs crumble bit by bit until high peaks are denuded of their elevation. This recognition propels the mind's eye to see beyond itself, which may be the reason why so many people are drawn to the wildness of mountains.

But why risk life and limb climbing icy rock walls, you might wonder? It's because they are mysterious, bewildering, and perilous. Although their vertical exaggerations provoke foreboding and horror, large mountains are dangerous more so for their weather than for their height. Sky-scraping mountains are about the deep secrets of winter, the punishing logic of cold air, avalanches, and glaciers. The serrated rock ridges that step up to the peaks of tall mountains are chiseled into statuary by icy whorls of violent wind, the freeze-and-thaw cycles of night and day, the avalanching of heavy snow pack, and the downward glide of glacial ice, all of these mere afterthoughts of severe and unremitting alpine weather. Strong winds and sub-zero temperatures at altitude are particularly punishing for mountaineers, able to freeze skin and render ice impenetrable to the blow of an axe and the bite of crampons.

Long ago in the remote Dry Valleys of Antarctica something special happened to me. It was mid December, the apogee of summer when temperatures hover between cold and very cold. There is no night at that time of year. Two of us were camped high in a misfit boulder valley that had melted out from under the ice cap, now several kilometers away. We were geologists at the bottom of the world, a peculiar place where south is squeezed down to a point and north is everywhere else.

This frozen place is desert where old snow is perpetually blown about. The month before on the messy rubble of a till plain not far from here, the two of us had traipsed up and down tall desert dunes, exquisite bedforms shaped like crescent moons resting on their sides. Incredibly, gravel, not grains of sand, held up their steep angles of repose. Near our tent, the tops of stones protruding above the frozen ground were shaped into irregular polygons by the searing power of wind-blown sand.

As we feared, the narrow valley where we were encamped turned out to be a luckless place. There, we endured a windstorm for two days, pinned down shoulder to shoulder in down sleeping bags, hardly moving as if mummified in death. Torrents of heavy air coursed off the ice sheet and slammed against the canvas walls of our green tent. The cold and desperate conditions alternately sharpened and dulled my uneasy mind.

At one point, my weathered thoughts conjured an aerial view. Wind packed with cold and snow swirled about in billowing eddies, moving over the ground so fast it seemed as if the daydream was caught in fast-forward mode. Every so often a lonely pinprick of green flickered through the whiteout of the ground. I tried to see myself down there in that canvas tent but couldn't. I opened my eyes and could.

Somehow, each blast of wind was rebuffed, thousands of them. How?

I cannot say other than we did nothing special to deserve that outcome. What was it like? W. H. Hudson described a madhouse of a windstorm in *Idle Days in Patagonia*. "And the winds are hissing, whimpering, whistling, muttering and murmuring, whining, wailing, howling, shrieking – all the inarticulate sounds uttered by man and beast in states of intense excitement, grief, terror, rage, and what not."

After the maelstrom, I wanted fresh air, lots of it, and space to breathe it in. My feelings needed sorting out. We both had to cry, but not together. I shouldered my rucksack and left, trudging upslope on lonely wind-packed snow. My destination some two kilometers away was a minor ridge in sharp shadow. I needed quiet time watching the polar icecap.

In no time at all, I reached a scree band at the foot of a sandstone ridge. The true and easy feel of my body's weight in motion exhilarated me. The air was dreadfully cold and dry. Scrambling awkwardly over piles of tottering boulders, I felt uneasy and at risk. Once on firm bedrock, however, the act of climbing relaxed me. Several hours later, a roof pendant in the cliff wall – an overhanging sill of rust-iron basalt – stopped me cold. Traversing carefully to my right along a narrow ledge jutting out into air, I soon encountered smooth ice filling a slash in the basalt sill.

This was the crux. With my shoulders tensed, I started up relying on my ice axe and crampons for purchase and "pied a plat" for balance, flat-footing my way up the slope. The ice was cold and brittle. Thousands of ice shards fell away, clinking like broken glass with each placement of my crampons. Panting hard from the exertion, I cut steps into two slabs of high-angled ice. Eventually, I reached a long vertical chimney of fractured rock running straight up to the top of the ridgeline. Relieved, I opened my parka and placed my frozen fingers on the hot, sweaty skin beneath my woolen shirt. Shivering slightly, I remember thinking how peculiar to inhabit a body simultaneously freezing and roasting. I laughed quietly, releasing my tension.

Once safely on the ridge crest, I looked south to the pole. No human had ever been here before. In front of me, an endless apron of frozen water, wider than ocean-wide was drowned in muted light. Honey-colored clouds front lit by the low sun were weakening. I stared into vastness, not memorizing, but clumsily folding the gripping view into my head. Not a breath of air anywhere, the measured hush absolutely still, containing nothing whatsoever to overhear.

Unnerved by the deadness of the moment, I turned away. Over my shoulder, I saw the crooked ridgeline and an endless spread of messy rocks and crusty snowfields. Everything, absolutely everything, was locked away in the graveyard of deep time. No smudges of lichen or moss, no blades of grass, only the carbonized impressions of Permian ferns splayed out on the bedding planes of thin shales. Nothing anywhere about was alive but me. Absolutely nothing. Somehow, I had not approached, but had passed through a portal where everything caused ache.

Not much later, the clouds drained the radiant light out of the polar ice and slowly fused the sky and ice into an immense expanse, a seamless wholeness, a world devoid of parts. The familiar sweep of space disappeared. My eyes forgot my mind. No horizon, no up or down, no inside or outside, no color, no sound, no smell, no time, no life, no memory, simply wide-openness filled with silence. The infinite underbelly of the cosmos had engulfed me, my solid body waned to no thing at all. Somehow, I was free falling into a vastness, the infinite, an unearthly void, a faceless enormity well beyond the clutch of words and rationality. I had unintentionally come upon my authentic self. I cried.

Gifts of darkness, solitude, and pain underscored by senseless mountains of stone and ice scraped me raw on that notable day of my life. I stood stripped of memory, dreams, and intellect. I encountered the unblemished clarity of raging nonexistence. The space separating mentalscapes from mountainscapes vanished. I was unmapped. There are Earth's stones and there are our concepts of stones. I've learned that deep non-presence is not story to tell, nor topographies to memorize. Its primal undershadow is beyond comprehension by Earth-bound minds preoccupied with yes and no, taking and giving, good and evil, living and dying.

Over a lifetime, that special involvement with the pervasive nothingness of mountains has hovered inside of me everywhere I have climbed. Whenever I have had shadowy thoughts of vanished seaways and colliding continents, the strangeness of these penetrating moments has settled agreeably, quieting my insides. The all-embracing intimacy of impermanence is the vital essence of all that was, is, and ever will be.

Yes, great, upright rocks in mountains fall apart without regret. The deep simplicity and completeness of that unvarying poetry, whereby everything matters and so nothing matters, infused my being. From mountains, I learned that I am simultaneously so much more, and so much less, than the human I appear to be.

UNSPARING TRUTH

"....should the truth about the world exist, it's bound to be nonhuman."
Joseph Brodsky, *On Grief and Reason: Essays*, 1995

Existence, since its beginning, has been deeply steeped in the poetic interplay of physics and chemistry. Together, physical-chemical processes vibrantly exfoliated into the geology and biology of our small planet. Named Earth, though mostly flooded by an ocean of water and wholly submerged in an ocean of air, our planet exudes the essence of deep time.

How can *Homo sapiens* ever claim to have access to the base revelations that have fired up the universe, including the peculiar life-giving mysteries of Earth? Being mere mortals, this human drive to understand absolutely is set against an impossibly steep and deep impasse, beyond which lies a domain not simply obscure, but utterly opaque and impenetrable. Yet, such mind-numbing hopelessness does not sit well with natural scientists, who proclaim that their methods of inquiry, based on observation, reason, and mathematics, can access the grave reality of the cosmos to some degree, perchance to a significant degree. But the critics of science point out that existence – all of it – is broadly and deeply complex, meaning that scientists, being all too human, will mistakenly misjudge the simplicity of their conclusions about the deep-rooted reality of Earth.

Most scientists, however, disagree with this pessimistic outlook. They counter that such pitfalls are ultimately avoidable in the long run, because the results of scientific work are only trusted if, at the end of the day, they have stood the rigor of critical judgment. By this I mean that all scientific claims, whether they are observational, experimental, or theoretical, are tested incessantly by direct attempts to disprove them.

Yes, the mettle of the scientific procedure is strapping skepticism, not the crippling sort espoused by die-hard cynics, but the disbelieving insights of open-eyed, clear-headed interrogators. "Is that what your claim is based on? I'm not impressed. Convince me that your findings are worth believing." Another might say: "If what you allege is correct, then this also has to be true. Let's see if it is." If the result of such challenges conflict with the proffered hypothesis, then the claim is judged to be lacking and duly modified or is considered to be bogus and thereby refuted and discarded.

The logical process of falsification as a means of revealing truth is slow and arduous, as well as inefficient. But it seems to be the only legitimate means we have devised so far to access the workings of the natural world as they are, rather than as we imagine them to be. Don't get me wrong. The human imagination is a precious human faculty, but it tends to conceptualize a fanciful world of personal sentiment, a reverie that has little to do with the hard-nosed reality that created the universe and birthed sundry life on a singular, solitary planet adrift in the vastness of space. Paradoxically, scientists seek truth obliquely by exposing untruth, in actual fact searching for a speck of gold in a riverbed by mining out thousands of tons of sand and gravel.

The scientific manner of investigating natural processes is tantamount to trying to complete a complicated jigsaw puzzle of the universe that has an infinite number of interlocking pieces. The puzzle solvers try to fit each piece, one by one, against the irregular edges of the parts of the jigsaw already put together. If it doesn't fit anywhere, the piece is set aside and others are tested in the very same way.

With dogged persistence, this step-by-step, trial-and-error procedure eventually yields a piece that dovetails smartly with a part of the assembled puzzle. No matter how snug the fit, however, the piece may not belong there, because it does not match up with the pictorial representation of the cosmos that is emerging as more of the puzzle is put together. If the piece does fit and does conform logically to the puzzle's image of the universe, then presumably it belongs there, in much the same way that the inability to falsify a scientific hypothesis despite repeated attempts at disproof indicates that the notion likely is an approximation of some aspect of absolute reality. In this way, nonhuman truths about the natural world, such as entropy, Boyle's law, evolution by natural selection, and global plate tectonics, are uncovered, intellectualized, and synthesized ever so carefully so that with time they glow forthrightly with simplicity, grace, and beauty.

What follows are explications of two general, yet focused, nonhuman truths revealed by scientific inquiry. As concepts go, their individual surfaces are quite austere, though beneath their patina they are deeply entwined and darkly shadowed. At depth, they transform, strangely enough, into nonhuman truth. The profundity of their complexity is what makes them especially germane to the 21st century.

Truth: The Universe Is Vast

Few will doubt the sensibility of the declaration that the cosmos is expansive beyond reason. After all, any person who gazes at the vaulted darkness of the night's sky will agonize over the never-ending obscurity that is up there. Yes, bits of starlight, the resplendent nuclear emissions of trillions of suns, burn fiery pinpricks into the inky nothingness of space. But despite this wondrous "candlelight of the gods," what is out there is mostly cold, empty, dark, and lifeless. It is desperately inhuman and it is terrifying. What can we make of this eternal, consuming darkness, looking at it from Earth, where life, thriving for billions of years under the warmth of its sun, has diversified into the opulence of today's biota, including you and me?

For obvious reasons, the sky has always fascinated humans. The mind's eye of early *Homo sapiens* must have recognized star patterns adrift in the heavens. Amazingly, familiar groupings of stars reappeared in the same section of the sky in a rhythmic pattern. These astronomical recurrences – the apparent birth, death, and rebirth of some constellations – enabled people to devise elaborate calendars that tracked reliably the passage of the seasons.

The endless repeatability of star clusters through time reassured people that the sky gods and spirit beings were reliable and trustworthy. Also, Earth appeared to be solid and unmoving, and so must be located at the center of the cosmos. Influenced by the aesthetic credo of Aristotle, Greek natural philosophers transposed the flawless geometric curve of the circle to the orbital motion of the Sun, the Moon, and the five known planets around an unmoving Earth. Ptolemy tirelessly incorporated "wheels within wheels within wheels" to account for the many new, detailed observations of the irregular trajectories of the planets. Regardless of such intricacies, everything essentially was as it should be in this geocentric depiction of the universe. Later, the Catholic Church stridently endorsed the worldview that Earth and its people were the focal point of existence, and this mistaken conviction endured as a dogmatic human truth for a few thousand years.

Serious misgivings about the efficacy of the geocentric model emerged in the sixteenth century. Relying on the logical truth of numbers and the latest astronomical observations, Nicholas Copernicus in his book *De Revolutionibus Orbium Coelestium* proposed that Earth was not riveted to the center of anything, but spun around its axis once each day and moved around the Sun once each year. In fact, all the known planets did likewise, but at different rotational and orbital rates. Furthermore, Copernicus insisted that the stars are much farther away from Earth than is the Sun. To put it bluntly, the nonhuman truth of reality discerned by mathematical logic indicated that Earth is located nowhere in particular.

This direct challenge to Church orthodoxy troubled the religious authorities. Despite the relentless persecution of heretics by the clergy, the coffin was nailed shut on the Western geocentric model of the Solar System by elegant intellectualism, notably Galileo's meticulous spyglass observations, Kepler's empirical laws of planetary motions, and Newton's gravitational theory. Yet, it took centuries of bitter, cruel conflict before the efficacy of scientific reasoning and mathematical insight could displace the deep convictions of religious faith.

This not so simple, nonhuman truth based on astronomical investigations is clear-cut: Earth's location in the vastness of space is quite unremarkable. The birthplace of humankind is nothing more than a trifling aggregation of Solar-System debris situated far from the galactic center of a spiral nebula, the Milky Way. To the disappointment of some, Earth has no special presence, nor significance, when viewed against the vast backdrop of space and its countless stars, wispy smudges of interstellar dust, and infinite volumes of emptiness. Yet, as far as we know, unlike any other place in the universe, Earth today is singularly redolent with complex forms of life, some thirty million species of microbes, plants, and animals, including *Homo sapiens*, a mélange of organisms self-organized into lively, complex communities, which biologists call ecosystems.

Truth: Humans are Animals

In the ancient Mediterranean countries, Greek scholars were astounded by the prodigious assortment of organisms that populated their world. Creatures, all manner of them, were everywhere. They lived in and on the ground, as well as in and on the bodies of others. They flew through air, pushed through water, crawled through mud, and scampered to the tops of trees and hillsides. They walked, slithered, wriggled, crept, backpedaled, skulked, and hopped about in deserts, grasslands, floodplains, forests, swamps, beaches, and the seabed during the light of day and the darkness of night, in rain and in snow. It was a gala of organic activity, altogether untidy, muddled, and bewildering to say the least.

Something needed to be done to clean up the messiness of it all. And so Plato and Aristotle obliged. Firmly believing in the everlasting forms of all organisms, the Greeks devised an all-inclusive, ranking order of existence, a magnificent Scala Naturae. In this formalized worldview, all known organisms were assigned a specific position on the Ladder of Nature commensurate with their taxonomy. The spare, blander plants – lichens, mosses, and ferns – were placed near the base of the hierarchy, just above inanimate stuff like stone and soil. Above them were the flowering plants with their patterned corollas and multihued blossoms. Higher up were the lowly invertebrates, spineless creatures like worms, snails, and insects, and over them the striking vertebrates as small as frogs and as large as elephants. Humans, the quintessence of organic perfection in this worldview, occupied the very top level of this elaborate schema.

This Great Chain of Being, a remarkable intellection of the world, made intuitive sense to the Greek logicians of the time who were preoccupied with what they believed to be levelheaded erudition. Scala Naturae, they reasoned, underscored the inborn condition of the world, and was a fitting tribute to the primacy of the rational human mind.

Building on this glorious proposition, the Papacy later beatified this pagan cosmology by ratcheting up the Ladder of Nature into the heavens. And by so doing, the profane was divined. True believers, perched high on this ecclesiastical Ladder of Nature above infidels, animals, plants, and rocks, gazed upward to the venerated Kingdom of God, populated by angels and overseen by the omnipotent, omniscient Creator of the universe. Finally, the cosmic order was complete: God, Angels, Man, and all the rest.

This static view of Godly creation was changed forever by Charles Darwin's *On the Origin of Species,* which was published in 1859. Long foreshadowed by the evolutionary speculations of others, Darwin's grand synthesis laid the groundwork for modern biology and ecology by proposing that Earth's biota, like its landscapes, changed routinely over time.

It became glaringly apparent to naturalists that both the living and nonliving parts of the world evolved in ways that are logically knowable: the rocks and their structures, according to James Hutton and Charles Lyell, were harbingers of colossal but slow geologic transformation of ancient geographies; and the fossil record, according to Charles Darwin and Alfred Wallace was the product of astonishing, incremental biological transformations. In other words, there is kinship among all present-day landscapes and their living communities of organisms, which together emerged step-by-step out of Earth's immense geologic past.

Speciation of all organisms, including *Homo sapiens*, resulted from co-evolution by natural selection, as seas retreated and advanced, mountains rose and crumbled, climates warmed and cooled, and species appeared and vanished across the eons. Evolution requires time, and there was plenty of it as finally revealed by the slow decay of radioisotopes in minerals and rocks. As some say, it took Earth four and a half billion years to discover that it is four-and-a-half-billion years old.

In this new materialist mindset, the implications for human origins became clear and far-reaching. The collective birthright of *Homo sapiens* was a scientific rather than a theological story, obscenely commonplace instead of supremely sanctified. Nature's perceived order is not at all like a well-crafted ladder with its secure rectilinear form and solidly fixed rungs, but is more akin to a rooted evolutionary tree with its ever-spreading entanglement of branches.

Evolutionary theory implies that people have deep geologic roots, and their genesis story was not merely a human one, but was a shared biological epic of co-evolution. Implausibly, humans were deemed by evolutionists to be mere animals to their very soul. It's little wonder that this new frame of mind was utterly reprehensible to the Church. After all, this was no longer simply about "real estate," nothing more than concessions about where Earth was located in the vastness of heaven. Rather, this heresy challenged a deeply held belief that the biosphere was supremely premeditated, willfully created and perfected by God specifically for habitation by humans.

All biological existence, now perceived to be the result of evolutionary vibrancy, became philosophically and metaphysically problematical. The nitty-gritty import of biological evolution by natural selection, it turned out, is grounded in chance and random occurrences, a robust, yet fortuitous blend of energy, molecules, continuities, chaos, and contingencies that somehow became alive and blindly unfurled into poetic webs of life. To add insult to injury, evolutionary biologists discovered that Nature has no compass, and in fact stumbles into the deep future without direction. Moreover, the world has no destination, no particular end point, no favored state of being; it simply becomes whatever it becomes. For humankind, the implications of this pointless biological materialization were sobering indeed. To state it tersely, the appearance of the animal species *Homo sapiens* was not godlike or intentional, but resulted from pure chance occurrences, from an eternal roll of dice.

As the literate populace of Europe and America pondered the 'one long argument' laid out by Darwin in his *Origin*, its existential implications exerted a vexing psychological and emotional burden on humans that persists today. What do these far-reaching evolutionary shenanigans imply about the self-esteem of human life, if all species, including our own, did not somehow pull themselves out of the primordial mud by the bootstraps? It's plain to those who see with the eyes of science that Nature, every bit of it, is the product of blind and arbitrary forces, an ever-changing arrangement of chaotic physical processes that operated across long durations of geologic time, instead of a static template of objects created by God. For all intents and purposes, Nature is an incorrigible groper and not a circumspect designer, despite its lushness, its diversity, its dynamism, its complexity, its multilayered organization, and its captivating beauty. What does this bode for the future of humankind?

It is clear to scientists that biological evolution relies exclusively on a simple, time-tested strategy: trial and error. Whatever doesn't work soon vanishes and something new eventually comes to light in its place.

Creation always requires destruction, for there is no other way for newness to materialize. Annie Dillard in *Pilgrim at Tinker Creek* discovered an unpleasant and unexplainable truth: "The faster death goes, the faster evolution goes." She, bemoaning this dire state of affairs for human existence, cries out: "Just think: in all the clean beautiful reaches of the solar system, our planet alone is a blot; our planet alone has death. I have to acknowledge that the sea is a cup of death and the land is a stained altar stone. We, the living, are survivors huddled on flotsam, existing on jetsam. We are escapees. We wake in terror, eat in hunger, sleep with a mouthful of blood."

Existence, billions of years old, can only be today what it has become, regardless of how we think it ought to be. Life demands death, and so individuals die and species go extinct. This truth – arrivals, farewells, and revivals – has been Earth's way since its beginning. The fuzzy looseness of the human mind-set is why the mythic contours of personal non-existence are easy to map, but hard to accept. I was not here forever, then briefly I am here, and some day afterward I will not be here forever. There is no give-and-take in the unfussiness of existence. For that reason, each of us must reconcile our life-long dreams and hopes with this nonhuman/human state of existence, a confusing inscrutable truth if there ever was one. The significance of this life-principle is startling. Death is a privilege, because it is the only way to be alive.

CREATION STORY

"It is as if a great wind has surged through everything, but a wind of no defined dimensions or direction, a wind that simply shapes the emptiness all around without touching anything."

Steve Sem-Sandberg, 2009, 2011, *The Emperor of Lies*

I recall my first geology field trip to the White Mountains of New Hampshire. That Saturday morning was flawless, with a crisp, cobalt blue sky, bold mountains surrounded everywhere by spiky trees, and late-fall sunshine caressing the deep-seated creek bottoms. Everything about the moment was sharp and meaningful.

We were hiking slowly to the top of a minor summit, whose name I've forgotten, to view how the topographic irregularities of the high peaks of northern New England had been sculpted by the flow of glacial ice. This – the stiff cold, the crystalline ice and snow, the messy glacial drift, the wind-tormented rock walls – was a world I craved to know.

I had spent much of my childhood devouring stories about remote wilderness, and while in high school had read and reread the classic mountaineering literature. I had pored over those in my town library, books like Edward Whymper's *Scrambles Amongst the Alps*, Maurice Herzog's *Annapurna*, Charles Houston and Robert Bates' *K2: The Savage Mountain* and, of course, Edmund Hillary's epical *High Adventure*.

The field excursion in northern New Hampshire was my very first foray into real mountains. I was no longer scurrying among the hill knobs near my home a few hours south of here, but ascending thickly shadowed ravines that opened up to brazen upsweeps of granite ledge.

Shadowed by Deep Time

About halfway up the footpath to the summit, my professor, a wizened, bespectacled man with thick fingers, stopped abruptly. He gazed at my feet and pointed to a tiny grain of sand that someone ahead of us had dislodged from the hard-packed ground. He looked directly into my eyes and whispered: "There's geology, Paul. Not the grain of quartz, mind you, but its tiny displacement. Make no mistake. That's what's important for you to understand." Without another word or gesture, he turned and trudged upward. I stood perfectly still, stunned, not because I comprehended what he had said – I had not – but because what I had heard him say sounded ridiculous.

Was it a joke? In my adolescent mind, geology was about Earth muscling everything into place. What intrigued me was the furious madness of volcanic blasts of ash, of seismically induced mudslides, of storm-shaped shorelines, of Himalayan-size avalanches; certainly not the submissiveness of a misshaped grain of silica. What an absurdity. I had a strong urge to kick that tiny bit of sand.

The apparent foolishness of my professor's words stayed with me over the years, lurching about in my sub-consciousness. Only after decades of pondering the value of landscapes have I come to appreciate what I was told that morning in the White Mountains of my youth. Miniscule, incremental changes repeated over hundreds of millions of years are the stuff from which Earth's Homeric sagas are realized. These accumulations of tiny moments that raise the muddy abyss of an ocean into the solid hugeness of jagged mountains never end. Remarkably, large effects are often, perhaps mostly, the result of repeated, undersized causes.

This seems preposterous to those unfamiliar with the doggedness of geologic forces operating over expansive sweeps of deep time. We modern humans are acutely visual creatures, and this proclivity to see rivets our mind on the material furnishings of the world: rivers with muddy shores that can be fished and dammed; plains carpeted with thick grass that can be grazed and plowed; forest tracts with pure stands of hardwood that can be harvested and suburbanized. But this is a sidelong glance at Nature, similar to what we do when we chance upon a naked torso of a life-size statue in a crowded museum and never risk taking a satisfying look at what really is there.

Nature is process through time and not, as most believe, objects in space. And so, slow, indistinct geologic processes outlive the firmness of individual mountains and humans alike, as both succumb to entropy and disaggregate into dust. Meanwhile the resilient processes flow onward long and strong, and create brand-new transfigurations of ridges, forests, and creatures from the rubble of the past. The callousness of this deep temporality is profound: Earth will have its way whether you are a stalwart mountain or a wondrous person. That, it seems to me, is a bedrock truth.

If you are unconvinced, go stand on the knurly rock outcrops that compose the flat, outstretched, eastern terrain of the Canadian Shield west of Quebec, Canada. The coarse-grained granites and gneisses of the region have an ashen pallor and are old, having endured billions of years of abuse from the elements. They have survived slow, incremental damage over the eons, like someone's skin being poked gently with a finger over and over until it begins to hurt, then bruises, and finally bleeds.

Walk eight kilometers straight on, stand back and swivel this distance upward into the sky, suffusing the airy space with massive rock. That is what once stood here in the Grenville Province of eastern Canada, a chain of mountains of Himalayan grandeur. What happened? It was nicked apart, morsel-by-morsel, by drops of rain and flakes of snow, and tyrannized by wind and glaciers until it was no more. The veritable Goliath dropped down flat by David's pebble, launched not by a hand sling but by unremitting cascades of air and water. Even more astonishing, there are exposed roots of several such decapitated mountain belts – each once tall and robust, all of them now buried side by side in the boggy, till-spattered graveyard of the Canadian Shield.

Few things die as slowly as mountains. These walls of up-thrust stone come and go. This is what it means to be part of the planet's chime, to exist within a tiny crevice of eternity, to be at the whim of the untiring force of gravity. Our human preoccupation with histories and stories, with their beginnings and their ends, with verbs and nouns, is illusionary, for these exigencies are concerns of the mind and not of the rain and the mud of Earth.

James Hutton, an eighteenth century Scotsman, knew this well. He wrote in *Theory of the Earth*, "…we find no vestige of a beginning – no prospect of an end." There are no promises beyond that actuality, no likelihood whatsoever for enduring existence in the cold silence of a snow pack or in the searing language of a burning star. Everything slips into oblivion by its own accord. Nothing that's left behind survives except as an unformed memory that vanishes in the blink of an eye.

This bracing truth is the way things are, but up to a point. Creation requires destruction. The two go hand in hand. Earth, like all planets, is materially finite. This means that newness, if it is to happen, must emerge from what already is.

Fresh chains of mountains are created by the impact of continents drifting along Earth's graceful curves. Wherever landmasses head butt, the volume of space that accommodates the seafloor between them deflates with time. The outcome is fated. The thick sedimentary accumulations in the ocean's abyss are grievously tectonized by the smash-up of colliding blocks of granitic crust riding on huge lithospheric plates. Those flat-lying blankets of marine mud and sand, derived from the erosion of old mountain belts that no longer exist, are crushed accordion style and once again thrust upward into a mountainscape.

It is slow anguish. At first, bruised swellings of the sea bottom are raised, dried of seawater, and vegetated by the butts of trees instead of the fronds of kelp. Imperceptibly, these forested hills gain altitude by the relentless compressive power of the continental pileup of tectonic plates that has been ongoing for thousands of millions of years. Eventually, parcels of the old, broken seabed are stranded on a mountain peak well above tree line and blasted by spindrift. Remarkably, the wet depths of Earth have become the icy tops of the world. These boundary-blurring tectonic cycles are pregnant with creative splendor.

What is under-appreciated is the repetitiveness of this extraordinary creation story. The countless grains of sand and mud in the deformed strata that buttress a young mountain ridge likely have lain this way before. They represent bits of stone chipped off alpine cliffs of a bygone age that have been swept into the ocean's abyss. And so the upload of fresh topography is accompanied by the download of old topography, tsunamis of stone cresting here and collapsing there as they drift around the world on lithospheric plates. Things are born and things die, and matter gets reused over and over in similar as well as in brand-new ways.

This grand cyclic procession, which transforms generations of oceans into generations of mountains, requires prodigious loads of energy. The power to propel continents and frame up mountains is derived from deep within Earth's interior, partly the primordial heat of the hot core, but mostly the radioactive decay of minerals in the planet's mantle. Once these sources of thermal energy are expended sometime deep into Earth's future, the continents will set down roots of mantle stone and remain locked forever in place. No new mountains will appear anywhere once the far horizon of Earth is in perpetual arthritic stasis. Flowing water and air will then sandpaper down the upsweeps of rock in the lingering highlands to a drab geographic flatness.

It's difficult to make sense of the fact that air, a mere gas, and water, a mere liquid, are so caustic that, working together, they can dismantle the rock-tough hardness of mountains. But it is undeniable. This immeasurable quality of fluid softness that can undercut the grave weight of granite seems unreasonable and, hence, unacceptable to us mortals, a species preoccupied with achieving self-determination and material wealth at the expense of landscapes everywhere.

The future is always derived from the rearrangement of the past. Living creatures are no exception. All things alive breathe at the expense of the environment, sapping nutrients, water, and energy from its fabric and disposing of waste into its vastness. Stuff goes in and stuff comes out. This sparse economy promotes extravagance, as living organisms continually discompose their surroundings in order to prolong their aliveness. There are no exceptions to this dynamic calculus of life. So plants eat rock, and animals eat plants and each other. Eventually living entities expire and provide dead stuff that is reconstituted by growing plants into fresh cells of living stuff. Or the dead stuff is swept into the sea, deposited with mud on the sea bottom, and eventually uplifted into a towering mountain where erosion releases its chemicals back into the environment to begin the biogeochemical cycles anew. This is the very reason why the evolution of new species requires the extinction of established species.

To contemplate with stoic equanimity the long-term prospects of our species on Earth is disturbingly straightforward. No matter the pretense, *Homo sapiens* and all of its creations will some day vanish forever. Put simply, the artifacts of our industrialized society – its towering steel-girded skyscrapers, its continent-girdling roadbeds, its monumental Mount Rushmore sculptures – will be ground down and worn away by wind and rain, the eroded bits spread out in a knee-high layer of deep-sea mud that will be crushed into the flanks of new mountain chains. That inconspicuous bed of marine mudstone, really no more than a smudge in a thick sedimentary sequence, will be our modest bequest to Earth's far-flung future as our artificial creations become dwarfed by unhurried geological processes and the enormity of deep time.

DESERT DREAMSCAPE

"When the silence of dusk replaces the day's speaking, the wonder still remains: we are justified. We are justified in the order of being, together with our kin, the trees, the boulders, the creatures as bearers of the miracle of the creation: that there is something, not nothing."

Erazim Kohak, 1984, *The Embers and the Stars*

One late afternoon of a sun-drenched day, I was driving alone from Laramie, heading west for Seminoe State Park, a mountainous expanse of desert that straddles the North Platte River in south central Wyoming. There, I was to meet a colleague and together we would help students become geologic mapmakers.

Reluctantly, I had flown out of the late-spring lushness of upstate New York that very morning. This bold season is a time when the fresh greenery of forests stirs the lean air and swallows up the empty, white spaces of winter. Foliage sprouts up as heavy-eyed roots reawaken to the delight of fresh beginnings, a wild splendor that nourishes the human soul and inspires dreams. Deciduous trees, standing tall and stoic, envelop themselves in leaves born of soil, water, and sunshine. The dry air of winter becomes the wet ecstasy of springtime, not yet bothered by what lies ahead. Inside a handful of days, the sober winter is a receding memory but for a few lingering snow patches in the deep woods. And so, the contrast could not have been greater as I stared through a windshield into the treeless lay of a blistered Wyoming.

The West, with its heroic sweep of empty land and open sky, distresses many easterners. Perhaps the power of vacant spaces unravels the soul of a

New Englander, tugging on it bit by bit into the bright glare of day. Here, human life seems to be an afterthought. The bowl of the sky, the dried-out streambeds, the weather-beaten homesteads are laid out wide open year-round. The land is parched and dusty, always in mourning. The few trees hereabout are mostly grizzled and burnt up. Razor sharp shadows stand perfectly still. The soil is thin and thirsty, and like the stony ledges, baked rock hard. The sage grows sparsely and tough, living on almost nothing. Draped over it all is a huge quiet. Occasionally, ponderous clouds unleash a violent afternoon rain. But more typically this austere desert landscape is about the heavy weight of stillness, an evocative language of estrangement and longing.

The empty openness of the Seminoe wilderness is inimical to the closed forests of the Northeast, which are self-absorbed with crowding and concealment. Untrammeled forests are fully shaded even in the white light of noon, shuttered up tight, except near marshy ponds and wherever rotting snags and deadfall have gashed the forest canopy, allowing a spot of sunshine to root itself into the moldy soil. Life here is frantic. It's about hurrying and doing, surging and swelling, a timeless striving for the forced intimacy of biological plenitude. Step off a forest path and the dark woods swallow you up whole. But it's not just the overstuffed thickets that fill the interiors of forests. Rippling through the deep woods is treetop patter, as unseen things everywhere break, fall, scamper, chirp, eat and are eaten. It's no wonder that my nephew's wife, a native Nebraskan prairie dweller, feels cramped, even crushed, by the profusion of thick forest growth.

What I store in memory as I drive is the contrast between forest and desert, stones and life, day and night, today and eternity. Stop daydreaming, I tell myself. I'm here, in Wyoming. Not home. So focus on the empty road.

The sharp peaks of the Seminoe Mountains are dead ahead, ripping themselves out of the lonely ground. Before long, the roadway rises and narrows, and soon switchbacks over bone-white ridges and fevered rock. I'm negotiating the inside edge of a deep ravine, a crude incision cut brutally into the mountain's muscular flank, exposing raw beds of stone.

Abruptly, I wrench the car off the roadbed and step out into the still day. The heat ripples the roughened ground. I remove my eyeglasses and the world blurs up obligingly because of my nearsightedness. Half seen in this way, the mountain rim loses meanness, and the shattered twists and turns of its ridgelines and rock walls get evened out, looking more like a dreamscape than an actual landscape.

There is value, even a bit of wisdom, in this myopic view. This manner of half seeing allows the genuine deportment of the rock to emerge out of the lithologic fussiness that drowns it in countless details and quirky facts. It is precisely this out-of-focus glimpse that allows the complex curvatures of the bedrock to be tucked away into the flatness of a geologic map. It takes substantial aging to appreciate the value of this oblique perspective. This magical ruse, the geologic 'squint,' is what my colleague and I are here to teach our students.

At dawn of the following day, the sun hangs coppery ribbons of light on the far ridgeline. Slowly, twilight grows the quiet desert land. The young sun now peeking over the mountain rim is already melting the far horizon. By eight o'clock, field parties of determined geology students are spread about the region's harsh light intent on making sense of its deformed rocks. By mid-morning, white heat presses down hard on the desert's stiffness. It's going to be a burdensome day all around.

My coworker and I decide to spend the day examining a cutaway view of the mountain's understructure by walking along the foot of a cliff that drops down onto the edge of a gravel road. Having read and talked about the Seminoes before the trip, we conceive of the region's large geologic frame as worn-down granite that shores up tired beds of sedimentary rock. But this is a mere half dream of what's actually here. We're sure of it. What we're intent on doing today is to nail solid planking to our perception of the bedrock's staging, filling it out with proper angles, curves, and geologic structures. And so we begin our walk through this open world.

Hour after hour, we size up rocks, mostly slowly, mostly silently. I try to hang on to sundry impressions about the land's temperament, convinced in midlife that the onslaught of reason ought to be assuaged by feelings. All the while, the air shimmers with yellow dust and drinks deeply from our skin. We hardly pause as we transcribe the complex geometry of rock units into simple geologic compositions that we sketch with care and color on our topographic maps. Somehow this creative act is extremely gratifying.

Later, eating lunch in the hot shade and gazing absentmindedly at sharp-edged boulders in a drywash, I think back through the long morning. Yes, we've done a lot of seeing and a bit of reckoning, all the while softening our rawboned impressions into geologic symbols. But what engages me lately, much more than the geometric disposition of outcrops, is the heavy mark of the land and its deep time breathing themselves into a person's body so that they become a seamless whole. This geologic lifeline is as real and splendid as blood and skin. Sadly, this fulsome sense of the actual world, this wider and wilder poetry of the self as stonework, has mostly vanished from our busy urban lives.

The weight of this conviction is what my life spent traipsing in wilderness has led me to. In truth, it's all that I now have of lasting value to share with students. The ones preoccupied with the facts of the land and an analytical manner of knowing will be disappointed with what I have to share with them. Most will be curious but unsure, even leery, about what it will cost them to embrace a world with no edges, no distinctions, no rankings, and no endings, a complex Earth that cannot be mapped in any real sense.

That evening, time grows dark, then cold. The Big Dipper, alone and aloof, spreads itself out across the glacial sky. Although tired and sunburned, I sip thick, black coffee and attend to the desert's stillness. I wait and listen to the evening's hush. Having lived for decades in the deep-shaded forest of central New York with its mossy boulders and tree boles, I've learned about the restorative power of death and decay, a prescription for balancing the organic vigor of woodlands. It's not clear to me whether this ecological perspective has value for the lean, wide-open radiance of this Wyoming desert. The sinew of this hard country, I gather, has more to do with the staying power of stony pluck than with the shouting ecstasy of biological excess. For me, the desert is not about delight or exaltation. It's about doggedness and grit. It takes time for a forest being to see wild deserts with honest eyes. But tonight, deep in hushed moonlight, I sense sharp solitude and lonely, far-off secrets.

The days that follow repeat one another exactly – a mix of hot, dusty, sullen brightness. We traipse over miles of archaic terrain, disturbing a few mule deer and even fewer humming birds. By week's end our group has concocted a credible tale rendered as an exquisite geologic map that throws out light onto the terrain's shadows. It turns out that this land of desert sunshine is a throwback to the dark side of wildness.

The layout of the bedrock hereabout is forthright. The oldest crust, a basement complex of rough-hewn gneisses and granites of Precambrian age, stretches out across the northern section of the parkland. At first sight, they seem spiritless and are slashed by slews of gully washes. Close up and to the touch, you cannot help but grieve for what these rocks have endured – ceaseless ill treatment beyond belief. They were here during the earliest stirrings of the world when life was not much more than primitive microbes. At the time, the Precambrian Earth, leaping and boiling with early adolescent yearnings, longed to test its mettle.

There was no rush mind you, but simply the relentless, vise-like application of strapping tectonic power, wielded tiny bit by tiny bit, for every second of every minute of every day for hundreds of millions of years. Implacable orogenic forces crushed these primal stones into a welt, bruising them so deeply that they swelled up into a towering mountain range. The aggrieved rocks, now perched high above the world, took solace in the coolness of the flowing sky. But over the eons, the violent purity of the high-alpine weather – its sun, rain, fog, sleet, snow, ice, and wind – wore away the towering peaks of broken stone crumb by crumb, scraping them down to their deep crustal roots until the surviving rocks were now no more gallant than the rolling hills of a hinterland.

Many rock bodies in this messy assemblage are mangled horribly, twisted into convoluted folds and splintered by countless fractures. Large fault lines shoot across the countryside, slicing the terrain into a rubble heap of shattered rock. In a few places, the gneisses partially melted and flowed away from the tectonic pressure that pinched them relentlessly. Later, seething magmas rising from the underground blistered and burnt the already damaged rock, forcibly injecting themselves as massive plutons of granite and tabular dikes of basalt.

The denuded rocks that crop out in road cuts to the north of Seminoe Reservoir preserve the raw vitality of that billion-year-old Precambrian existence. There, gnarly granites and gneisses lie quietly, tight-lipped about their grueling, long-suffered geologic memories. Nonetheless, their grisly, malformed exteriors betray them, in much the same way that the deeply wrinkled skin of an old man's face reveals the expressive wonder of a long-lived life.

Farther south, unfinished Paleozoic and Mesozoic strata bury the gaunt shapes of the basement rocks. Stacks of the repetitive assortment of this sedimentary cover – sandstone, shale, and limestone – are piled one atop the other. Most days, the hot Wyoming sky cooks these rock sequences firebrick hard, though long ago it was entirely different. Most of these sedimentary beds started out as soft settlings of sand and silt grains in the cool, level water of a now long-gone seaway. Then a tectonic upheaval during the Cretaceous Period lifted them dripping wet and shoved them hard against the distended belly of the Rocky Mountains. Turned on edge like a fallen pile of books, the naked, heavy fringes of these tilted beds were cut into by sluicing water. The layers of soft shale were cut back into deep-dark slashes of dusty ground. In contrast, beds of hard-nosed sandstone and limestone stood up to the seasons, refusing to be eroded down to Earth's dark underworld. And so these resistant strata remain defiant, shoving their jagged edges into the sky.

Seeking escape one day, we stand quietly under the silence of the soil-littered shale beds that lie low and scabby between parallel rows of up-tilted sandstones. These cuestas rise above us like canted rooftops that lie side by side and mold themselves to the soft curves of the globed Earth. Here, the blazing sun lets no tree grow, yet the tired gray soil and broken rock are splattered with notes of splendor, thousands of tiny sweet-smelling, apple-red blossoms of ground-hugging cacti. We stand awhile and ponder the solemn beauty before us. Slowly, the timeworn stones become intimately joined to the cactus bloom and us, an emergent moment of a living circumstance that should never have occurred, but did.

We traipse into the late afternoon. Hour after blistering hour, the steep-angled shoulders of ridgelines confine the movement of our bodies and minds to the easy, limitless run of the shale-floored valleys, an open-ended expanse of spaces within spaces that brings to mind an impossible Escher creation. It takes my breath away.

Now back at camp just before the dead of night when our DNA and pretenses fade out, my book thoughts of daylight give way to elemental darkness. At such authentic moments, I become purely rather than seemingly human, as the deep wilderness night construes my DNA rather than the other way around. The still blackness of the night dissolves everything out of existence, and so the open leanness of the Wyoming desert becomes indistinguishable from the closed-in lushness of the New York forest.

When dawn opens the new day, does it matter whether contrasts in age and distance are large or small? It does, of course, to those who hold simply and tightly to a binary reality of desert and forest, of day and night, of you and me, of long ago and long to come.

Two weeks later, driving home on Interstate 80, I wonder what the desert's scorched terrain has taught me. I gaze flat out at the vanishing point of the roadbed, an undeviating line of reasoning scraped onto the twisted ground and made to fit our engineered future. There is the measured, ever-present whine of steel-belted tires, punctured now and then by the blare of car horns. Meanwhile, the enclosed space of our speeding van gets overfilled with muddy student prattle and their tongue-tied dozing, the commotion sloshing back and forth as regularly and frequently as the hissing swash and backwash of beach surf. Suddenly, I'm exhausted. Far off outside, a turbulent wind buffets us awkwardly along the exquisite linearity of the expressway. The world is big and takes its time, and is filled with chancy circumstances.

The wide drama of this desert land, polished smooth by ancient memory and blown empty by the wind, overwhelms our flat, cocksure thoughts that people alone grieve and howl. No matter our needs and wants, our matter-of-fact philosophies, our exact distinctions and prescriptions, our children's dreams. These human moments do not have much bearing when viewed against the enormity of deep time. What is relevant finally is the patterned bedrock that we construe as "deaf and dumb."

At day's end, it matters little that we have constructed a geologic map and that our economies and technologies have progressed so far and so fast, as we strive with fury to raise ourselves above the wild, unpretentious carelessness of the natural chaos that surrounds us. After all is thought and done, this solid hunk of continent beneath our rolling van wheels continues to drift about slowly on a tectonic plate that is going nowhere in particular. So, let's give praise for what's to come, whatever that might be, and seek silent answers to questions that cannot be worded.

VITALITY OF STONE

"More and more I'm trying not to look back at who I was, or even who I am, but the land itself. I am trying to let the land tell me who and what I am – trying to let it pace and direct me, until it is as if I have become a part of it."

Rick Bass, 2006, *The Lives of Rocks: Stories*

In the words of Rick Bass, we discover an obtuse view of the world that is filled with startling overtones about what is and what is not alive. In particular, it calls into question the reasonability of the claim that the vitality of existence, this force that we call life, resides exclusively in living organisms. Couldn't the breath of life be supremely bigger, broader, and more diffuse than mere cells, tissues, and beating hearts? This is the question that has saltated in the bower of my mind until its scabrous edges have become as smooth as rosary beads. Where truly does the rawness of life lie?

One day, decades ago, I felt sure that I encountered rock at the borderline of life. I was walking steadily up the dry wash of a streambed in the low mountains west of Tucson, looking at unfamiliar blossoms and jittery butterflies, dodging wasps along the way. I was alone. My plan was to get high up into the dry creek's headwaters. There is no finer geologic primer than wandering long and far over fresh ground created by riled-up river water. I've discovered that my obdurate mind wanders clean and clear in the open lean of stark, wide-open spaces.

Hours later, the loopy river channel secreted itself into the corset bindings of a gulch. Here, the pinched channel became a sluiceway packed with flood-tumbled rubble. The gully's bottom was not built upright by dropping smooth blankets of alluvium, but was roughly eroded out of obstinate rock, as if Orion's sword had disemboweled the mountainside. Large broken chunks of yellow sandstone hung half in and half out of the gully's shoulders. The going got tougher. For a long moment, I thought to quit but didn't. As I gained altitude while getting deeper into the vast space of the mountain's gully and its layered stones, I felt tangled emotions.

Late that afternoon, judging from the leaning sun and the swing of my shadow, I encountered a geologic oddity, a dogleg in the canyon's track. I veered sharply right with the twist of the gully, thought better of pressing on, and weary from exertion, sat down on a dry, creek-bed boulder. A single cloud shadowed the undisturbed stillness. I felt undersized. A deep-felt homage for the patchwork of the undistinguished perfection of this desert land overcame me.

A thin cluster of waist-high trees, twisted and thirsty, grew out of a curved, stone fracture on the far sidewall of the gully. In one arthritic tree branch, a blot of pure crimson, redder than the reddest apple, caught my eye. The red spot moved slightly, or so I thought, wavering in the heat shimmer coming off the baked stones. What is it exactly? Wanting to be noticed, the red spot leaped off the branch and flew straight at me and then veered away. Taken aback, I jumped up, shaded my eyes from the sun's glare, and followed the blood red, laser light whiz through the air and refract down the canyon. A cardinal, a red cardinal in the desert! Incredible!

Seconds later, I sensed something over my right shoulder, on the far side of the gulch bed above the slide-rock. I swung around and lifted my eyes to the high, mangled trees rooted to a scoured hollow of the cliff. The lone red fruit was gone, the daylight dulled by its absence. In the thin shade of those dwarfish trees was a messy pile of deadwood. One piece stared back, mouth cracked open, tongue sweating, eyes unblinking. It was a coyote. We held the gaze long and hard, minutes that were ours alone, a stretch of silence packed with faraway echoes. I scarcely breathed. Satisfied, perhaps bored or hungry, the coyote finally looked away. Then, she got up, stretched her dusty forelegs, and loped off quietly into the imperturbable stillness of the landscape. The moment's flow-lines come and go in the tiny breath of an instant.

The late afternoon relaxed into stony quietness. The sun went in and out of scud clouds and seemed weary of the day. Thoughts, unhinged from my mind, slid down the steep pitch of a rock slab. I glanced up absentmindedly at the bent trees flowering from the rock face. Unexpectedly, I sensed a secret of the world: *life resides in the hardness of the ground*. These outcrops of sandstone, these scree bands and creek boulders, are as alive as I am. The signs are all around me. We have it back to front. Life is dirt, slag, and mud. The magnificence and mutability of biological life, its strength and beauty, its resiliency and sensuality, are gathered from the rock of dark ridges and from the soil of flat ground. The copse of trees gracing the gully's sidewall is a declaration of the rock's aliveness, a fabric of living stories that connects this solid mountain to the brazen sky and blazing sun, and to the rhythmic prose of this essay.

Stones extrapolate themselves into trees and by so doing unify the ecosystem by the diffusion of its life force into all of its commingled parts. Here in this dry gulch, the grainy sandstone pale as garlic expanded its palette and sent a flushed glow into the heavens on the paired wings of a cardinal. Just minutes ago some of the rock's gritty life scampered along a ledge on the legs of a coyote. Shortly, flecks of quartz and feldspar will travel downstream in the body and thoughts of this biped. As penned by Robinson Jeffers, humans are "born of the rock and the air." I had once again become unwound.

Since that day, my wanderings among the peculiar rock alignments of mountain ridges have released deep-gut secrets about the ferocity of life and its connections to stone. By letting go of what's familiar, I sense the muffled stillness and the fecund staleness of bedrock crevices – bloated eons of it – that slow the wind and steep the day.

There, alone and uneasy, twisting and turning, half dreaming, I stare long at these ancient beds of rock and their fossil inhabitants. My stony forbears look straight at me unblinking. Under their fixed gaze, I finally crack apart and glimpse a feral self. In nothing flat, a fierce sensation of pure feeling, a lopsided knowing of the real, leads me by slow degrees further into myself than I ever thought possible. Hard questions are quiet and never easy to come by, and too far-reaching for words. They fall where they will, smarting and stinging. By now I have learned to accept the slow undertows of my questions, which swirl about as eddies, flooding time and distance.

This manner of knowing concerns feeling more than thinking. It is a kind of fierce awakening from deep inside that overshadows mere reason. Because of such experiences, truth as something felt has entered deeply into my consciousness so that I no longer ignore it. Shimmering sun, streaming air, surging creek, age-rusted sandstones, stiffened fossils are bone of my bone. All of this lives deep in the memory of my genes that I carry, giving form and shape to my flesh and thoughts. Remarkably, all the crackling meaning of life grows out of common stone, out of a presence not of our time.

This is as real for the blackberry patch and the wolf pack as it is for you and for me. The stiff-necked framing of the here and now will vanish suddenly and be replaced anew in the long time to come. This lavish windfall of reality, far too thick with significance to be agreeable, is cached in every single gouged-out rock of Earth and in every DNA molecule of humans. This multifaceted truth, the timelessness and wholeness of geologic and biologic entanglements forever changing, eclipses all of our human constructs, actual and imagined.

Consider the vital essence of a thing that is alive, the internal, self-maintained stimuli that fire up the deadness of its matter so that it lives imperturbably in defiance of entropy and makes more of itself effortlessly. What do I mean exactly when I declare that I was born into the world? Obviously, my beginning differs fundamentally from the inception of an ocean basin, the uplift of a mountain belt, or the formation of a glacier, because I was brought into this world gulping air and metabolizing earnestly, whereas these other things were not. Given that organisms and life indubitably are one and the same, the broad expanse of the Pacific Ocean, the crystalline basement of the Appalachian Mountains, and the ice fields of Mount Blanc exist, but do not have even a tinge of weighty, biological sigh.

But is this strictly true, I wonder? What exactly distinguishes living creatures from non-living stuff? What exactly differentiates a growing tree from the musty soil and the cracked bedrock beneath its roots, from the ruffled air of its leafy canopy? Does my heartbeat simply end at my fingertips?

Common-sense biologists, invested in straight-ahead thinking, dismiss such outrageous perplexity. After all, they point out, profound existence that we call life is compressed into the lush, elastic foreground of ecosystems, where communities of bugs, weeds, and beasts live out hard and sprightly allegiances as if there is no tomorrow. Ultimately all of this biological exuberance is killed or dies, and then rots, a necessary ecological habit that provides nutriment for other life in perpetuity. This repetitious renewal of the community's ecological fabric stands out brashly against the unadorned staging of the physical environment, a greenless, bedraggled framework of soil, bedrock, and landforms that cannot for long endure even the vicissitudes of wild weather.

To me, this binary model of reality – animate or inanimate – is a map without color and draft, which casts the ecological contours of the world into flat tones and blurry shadows. According to this schema, the pattern of the world is quite explicit. There is a prideful biota flame-lit with vitality that grows out of a disinterested habitat of lackluster deadness. The disjuncture between spirited and lifeless existence could not be rendered more grandly than in this dominate worldview.

Currently, research on the nonlinear, emergent complexity of systems has deepened our understanding of the natural world, especially its ecological alliances. According to this new formulation of reality, webs of life conduct their affairs far from equilibrium, poised precariously like a unicycle rider on a tightrope between order and disorder. Over the long run, this nervous tautness between things and activities is crucial for sustaining dynamic interactions within all levels of an ecosystem's menagerie of creatures. No single one could exist otherwise. Also, self-adapted ecosystems are not closed tight like the clamped shells of intertidal mussels at low water, but are open wide and loose to the weight and fire of the world at large, to the biochemical wizardry that slides down gradients of energy and matter. Most importantly, the classical dissection of the ecosphere into biotic and abiotic elements is considered to be not merely problematical but untenable, because responses to physical disturbance depend on the specific local ecological entanglements between organisms and the landscape. The two are inseparable.

This continuous interplay at the edge of criticality between biological diversity and landscape matrices is a far cry from the conventional models of ecosystems based on mechanistic doctrines of linearity, cause and effect, stability, balance, and discrete biological units marked by crisply-honed edges. Ecologists who favor the new paradigm consider the dualistic portrayal of the natural world as one part beast and one part rock to be unreasonably simplified or, more likely, groundless illusion. As quipped by Albert Einstein, "Things should be made as simple as possible, but not simpler." Such words give reason to pause.

If the principles of complexity have something to do with the way nature actually works, then what exactly goes into the mix of life? Think about a cell that is imbedded in the tissue of an organ of an organism that lives in a population of a community spread out across the nuanced, geologic and ecologic complexities of a landscape. Where exactly does the life force reside in such a nested arrangement of systems, all of them interdependent and interconnected at sundry scales of time and space, the entire mixture in a continual state of geoecological and evolutionary flux?

Is it possible that life is a peculiar blend of air, water, soil, rock and organisms? After all, a creature could not be alive without the infusion of all that "dead" stuff. Aren't the ecological transactions absolutely fundamental to the identity and very survival of each and every living organism? If so, then don't all the ecological ingredients comprise the primal jelly that generates aliveness everywhere in the world? Isn't it the system in its entirety that is alive and not merely the vegetated ground cover of the foreground and its adapted fauna.

Many, perhaps most, scientists dismiss such thoughts as farcical nonsense, no more actual than the dreamy perceptions of young children or, worse yet, the beastly animism of "primitives." Without doubt, such flights of fancy can succor the creative urges of artists and poets, but not scientists, they insist. After all, reality is no more or less than what it really is.

Organisms are alive; they live until they die. Air, water, and stones are neither natal, nor mortal; they simply exist. Yet, evolutionary biologists and paleontologists declare that inert molecules learned the dance of life in some early Precambrian sea. There was a moment when tiny particles of clay existed placidly as always and in a heartbeat they acquired the heft of life and now were able to die. And so bits of rock somehow pushed up the fullness of life from nothing at all. Since then, in the view of modern biology, sand and mud have become unearthly still, empty-handed so to speak, written away as heaps of broken stone without voice or dreams. Such are the habits of the mind once an unchallenged belief hardens into doctrine.

The more I pondered the perceptual consequences of life superseding organisms, the more convinced I became of its virtue. Over the years, I met a few deep ecologists with whom I shared my persuasion that rocks have heartbeats, that physical landscapes are the sinew of life. Belief in the undifferentiated finitude of life, I explained, distorts the reality of the living world.

Their reactions were predictably of one mind. In their view, I was merely invoking the Gaia hypothesis, James Lovelock's vision of Earth as a superorganism. But I was not, because unlike Lovelock I do not conceive the planet as a superorganism, but as a self-organized suprasystem of life. There is no doubt whatsoever that a living creature has life, but the quality and source of its aliveness are derived from the bedrock structure of the physical world from which it emerged. According to Adrienne Rich, "When it all stands clear you come to love the place you are...." It's been that way since the door of creation opened, when in a split second empty stillness poised at the edge of fire transformed itself into imagination and memory.

One evening while browsing through library journals, I came across a short article written by the Canadian plant ecologist J. Stan Rowe. Rowe takes issue with the arresting cornerstone of biology that life resides exclusively inside the organism, the result, he asserts, of "a faulty inside-the-system view." Rowe asks the reader to imagine instructing a student to examine plant tissue under the lens of a microscope. The blown-up field of view affixed at eye level will reveal cells gated by walls that, according to the biophysicist Harold Morowitz, are "...the closure of an amphiphilic bilayer membrane into a vesicle that represents discrete transition from nonlife to life." In this view, the cell wall resolutely impounds a capsule of life, a jerry-built chamber with a stout nucleus, coursing cytoplasm, colorful plastids, bits of mitochondria and other intriguing sorts of organelles, a salty stew red-hot with vitality.

Now, Rowe implores, take a fanciful field trip into the cell's interior spaces by shrinking yourself down to nanometer size. "What do you see?" asks Rowe. He answers: "Sight from within particularizes; lacking the outside perspective that reveals the whole, the student will see the cell contents as separate and unconnected objects. He or she might then logically identify the dividing, reproducing organelles as alive and their cytoplasmic matrix, vacuoles, and plasma membrane as dead. The idea that the totality is alive, so obvious from the outside, is not apparent." This, Rowe maintains, is the perspective we bring to the ecosphere, because we are "….deep-air animals living at the phase boundaries where air and water meet land, mistakenly identifying all manner of things as organic and inorganic, biotic and abiotic, animate and inanimate, living and dead. Dictionaries full of nouns show the efficiency with which we have thought the world to pieces."

Recently while walking the long slope of a logging trail in the ten-thousand-acre State Forest that abuts my home in central New York State, I was thinking about Stan Rowe's contentious proposal that life forces are not confined to organisms. I paused at a road cut of mangy shale, its beds tilted slightly off center. The day was grayer than the stone, breezes whispering through the forest growth, light rain muddying the roadbed and streaking my glasses. The air was warm, but I was cold. The crooked sweep of the road bank framed the fractured profile of the outcrop, which jutted uphill. At the base of the stone face, a drainage ditch choked with leaf and branch litter gurgled, as a thin stream of water, smelling sour, left for elsewhere. The twisted tree trunks of second-generation growth groaned quietly as their stiff limbs swayed with the wind, which was mostly kept aloft and loose by the forest canopy. A pair of tree stumps, knee-high and soaking wet, sat still among chicory, scrub and thistle, uncomplaining.

It was the sort of setting that invited deep contemplation. And so I indulged the moment and myself as part of that moment. Minutes later, I found my left hand clutching the base of a sapling, a sugar maple, growing in the thin soil smeared over the bedrock's roughness. Impulsively, I touched the gritty stone with my other hand, closing the circle of life – shale to maple to human to shale. The rat-tat-tat of a woodpecker and then the swish-swish-swish of wing beats punctuated the tranquility of the forest. Gray, wet light misted down on us all. It is the sensuous immersion in such unlikely moments, when the world gets turned over so that maps get lost, that the aliveness of the whole is sensed and internalized into the soul.

It is then that I receive rather than take; there's a difference, an authentic difference, between those two deportments as there is between those who section the world into discrete parts and those who do not. The complexities that are life – their energy, matter, and time that flow out of stone – infuse dark hillsides and dripping creek beds with extraordinary biological possibility. Gary Snyder said it well. "As the crickets' soft autumn hum is to us, so are we to the trees as are they to the rocks and the hills." This is the bedrock of all Earthly existence.

CATASTROPHISM

"History resists an ending as surely as nature abhors a vacuum; the narrative of our days is a run-on-sentence, every full stop a comma in embryo. But more: like thought, like water, history is fluid, unpredictable, dangerous. It leaps and surges and doubles back, cuts unpredictable channels, surfaces suddenly in places no one would expect."

Nick Slouka, 2010, "Hitler's Couch", in *Essays in the Nick of Time: Reflections and Refutations*

The word catastrophe rolls off a tongue heavy sounding for good reason. *Cata*, a Greek prefix meaning 'against' or 'back,' when joined to *strophe*, a Greek root denoting 'turning,' signifies something ominous, literally a turning back or a turning against. Dictionary definitions of catastrophe go something like this: "a disaster that leads to great loss of life" or "a violent change in the Earth's crust caused by earthquakes, volcanic eruptions, floods, or other natural processes." Its synonyms – devastation, calamity, upheaval, cataclysm, and the like – are equally menacing. There's no doubt about its purport whatsoever. The expression catastrophe bodes ill and does harm on a colossal scale. And yet this word of doom kept popping into my head on a tranquil day aglow with Australian sunshine.

Let me explain the source of my angst. I'm listening to Ted Bryant, a coastal geomorphologist and current Head of the School of Geosciences at the University of Wollongong tell a story. A group of us are standing on the flat lip of a sandstone rock face that drops steeply into the Tasman Sea. Enormous breakers are smashing themselves against the cliff base far below us, and the froth of the fluid turbulence bleaches out the cobalt blueness of the water. The rock parapet is durable and keeps the water at bay. We are safe from harm despite the rough violence below, and still my mind locks itself onto the word "catastrophe."

Ted scampers across a rubble heap of sandstone blocks and climbs atop a flat ledge of rock. He waits impatiently, hands tucked into pant pockets. He motions us to join him. "Now," he says "you can see it clearly." And he is right on two counts. I see it and it is obvious, even though it happened thousands of years ago.

We look intently at a rubble pile of boulders, pondering the meaning of what was plain to see atop the thirty-three-meter high cliffs on the north side of Mermaids Inlet in Jervis Bay, New South Wales. At first glance, there's nothing exceptional about the blocky boulders of sandstone, except that they are quite large, up to two meters long, and very heavy, a few most surely weighing a hundred tons. What does draw the eye is their dramatic positioning. They are not strewn about haphazardly, but are elegantly imbricated, leaning hard and heavy on each other's shoulders like a line of overlapping roof tiles or, as Ted puts it, "like fallen dominoes."

This orderly *en echelon* arrangement of stones is a clear indication of transport by moving water, even though they are perched on an isolated ridge high above the sea and weigh tons. A muscular current must have ripped off these mammoth slabs of sandstone from the top of these bedrock cliffs, carried them as bedload, and set them down in graceful imbricated patterns. Judging from the alignment, the current flowed to the northwest, a compass bearing that just about parallels the regional trend of the coastline.

"We're standing at thirty-three meters above high water," Ted reminds us. Wind-created waves, even the largest ones, cannot reach more than ten meters or so above the high tide datum, even when a storm surge rides on the back of a spring high tide. So, what could possibly have produced the distinctive imbrication of this rubble stack? What's truly remarkable is that this imbricated boulder pile is not unique to Mermaids Inlet, but occurs here and there along a four-hundred-kilometer stretch of Australia's rocky seaside.

Satisfied that we sense something far-reaching, Ted heads south, away from the midday sun, and scurries down a series of knee-high benches of roughened sandstone towards the tidewater of the inlet. We follow as the wind, dank and salty, freshens out of the east and the sky darkens with onrushing scud.

Soon, we reach a lip of rock at the inlet's edge and can go no farther. Waves at the cliff base hiss, as they surge into a small, tapering arm of the inlet. A magnificent vertical rock face of interbedded sandstones and siltstones faces us across a narrow bight of water. The sand layers are stiff and steadfast; the silt layers are not. As a consequence, the cliff face has weathered unevenly over time into a striking bas-relief composition. Level bands of ochre sandstone project out boldly from the cliff face and glow oddly in the stippled sunlight; they alternate with stripes of pitch-black darkness, the shadowy hiding places of the hollowed-out siltstones.

This series of marine sediments documents the repeated back-and-forth shifts of an ancient shoreline that was unable to rest easily at one location for a drawn-out period of time. The sand beds are wave-washed, shallow-water accumulations, the silt layers quiet, deeper-water deposits; both are now compacted and been shoved out of the sea. In effect, these alternating layers of sandstone and siltstone that outcrop in the cliff face are a tape recording, so to speak, of repeated sea-level fluctuations during a portion of the Permian Period. The water got deeper, then shallower, then deeper, then shallower, a mantra repeated over and over as the zero-contour datum advanced and retreated.

Ted, exasperated with our reveries about the seesawing shoreline, reminds us of the purpose of this field excursion. And so we move obediently to our right in order to get a better overview of the narrow headwaters of the inlet. This is where it must be important to be; we stop and examine what's far below us.

Tucked smartly inside an isolated arm of the inlet is a small pocket beach of clean sand. Fronting it and lying in a few meters of cold water is a pile of enormous tabular blocks, ranging from one to five meters in length and weighing hundreds of tons, the bigger chunks perhaps approaching a thousand tons. They clearly have been plucked out of the nearby cliff exposures, judging from their lithology and overall appearance. They seem to have been jammed into the narrow neck of the inlet. Although some of the boulders in the stack are imbricated, most of them don't seem to be. Ted points out that several of the larger blocks of sandstone have been flipped over onto their backs with their tops down and bottoms up.

According to Ted, this debris plug consists of huge boulders that were ripped off the sides of the headland and transported by a concentrated flow of high-velocity water. Given that even the largest storm waves are incapable of such a prodigious feat, what could possibly have created this mammoth rubble pile?

We retrace our steps back to the far side of the headland away from the water. A light, chilly rain is wetting the rock. We skirt a high ledge and stop at the entrance of what looks like a cave, but in fact is a long tunnel, the Gosangs Tunnel. This is not an ordinary kind of underground chamber that forms by dissolving limestone; rather it's bored into country rock made of tough, quartz-pebble sandstone. Oddly, both its entrance and exit are perched about twenty meters above the sea.

I wait as the others, led by Ted, crawl crablike into the opening and get swallowed up, one by one, by the tunnel's darkness. I stay behind and enjoy momentary solitude.

The subterranean passage leads my companions to the far side of the promontory onto a cliff terrace that faces out onto the expansive Tasman Sea. The scenery, they tell me later, is spectacular, so primitively stunning that it's painful to look at it directly. What's peculiar, however, is that the tunnel is clean of debris, almost spotless. It should be littered with cobbles and boulders of the surrounding quartz-sandstone rock. But it isn't. The tunnel is so tidy that it looks as if some giant creature blew out the debris, the way that a child blows out the contents of a straw plugged with the thick creaminess of chocolate malt. Where did the lungpower come from to rid the tunnel of its coarse rock rubble?

The afternoon is spent examining a coastal landscape that seems to have been ravaged by violence. We see sheared cliff faces and planed platforms of basalt and sandstone, channels carved across headlands and swept bare of debris, the cockscomb profile of Cathedral Rocks, incipient caves and perched sea arches, the Blowhole and Little Blowhole tunnels, fluted ramps and potholes scoured into hard rock, heaps of imbricated boulders, large angular stones jammed hard into the crevice of a rock ramp, and forty meters high on Minnamurra Headland an unsorted 'dump' pile of mud, sand, and boulders that remarkably includes the fragments of seashells.

There is no doubt whatsoever. The southern coastal border of New South Wales is a battered landscape. Its eyes are blackened, its limbs broken, and its torso brutalized. It's bewildering, even unsettling, to see landforms maltreated in this way. A mad, wild thing has happened here. Ted and his research colleagues believe that they've identified the culprit that laid waste to this stretch of seaboard. They claim that for the past six thousand years towering walls of water, tsunamis, have repeatedly smashed into the seascape of New South Wales.

As you might imagine, this assertion flies in the face of geologic orthodoxy. Coastal landforms and their deposits, most earth scientists believe, are the handiwork of waves, tides, and currents, the result of systematic erosion and accretion that create sea cliffs, wave-cut platforms, and sand beaches. Not true, declares Ted in his recent book *Tsunami: The Underrated Hazard*. "Use your eyes and look for yourself at the destruction that is all about you," he urges anyone who comes out in the field with him. "It's undeniable and as clear as the nose on your face."

Much of the southeastern shoreline of Australia has not evolved slowly and routinely as the orderly models of coastal development proclaim, Ted insists. Rather, this coastal stretch is the brainchild of dementia, at the very least frenzied idiocy. A series of tsunamis, at least six of them in the past six thousand years or so, have brutally smashed over and through the resistant bedrock headlands of southern New South Wales.

One massive wall of water, a mega-tsunami, managed to overtop a promontory in Jervis Bay that rises 130 meters out of the sea. Look down the length of a football field from one end of the safety zone to the other. Now use your imagination and raise it on end so that it reaches the sky. No doubt about it. This is about catastrophe, the very word that dismays most geologists, causing them to grimace and reach for antacid tablets.

Such a response seems a bit odd with tones of obscurantism, does it not? However, this uneasiness with cataclysmic accounts of Earth's history has a long-standing tradition in modern geology, and is a reaction against the strong-arm tactics of the seventeenth- and eighteenth-century Protestant Church to impose Divine rightness onto Earth's history.

It took centuries for the discipline of geology to unburden itself of the beguiling conviction that Earth's landscape was created about six thousand years ago. This notion of a young Earth was propounded and scrupulously upheld by theologians, who were the cultured men of God, natural philosophers who interpreted Earth in accordance with the sacred truths of the Bible. And so, the six days of the Genesis story were understood, in a more worldly-wise manner, to symbolize six time "eras," each terminated by a catastrophe, the most recent being Noah's Deluge unleashed by God to punish humankind for its sins.

The brevity of Earth's age required that all of its vast oceans, its uplifted and tortured mountains, its numerous crystalline and layered continental rocks, and its diverse plants and animals be understood as arising from cataclysmic acts of God. As such, Earth's rocks were reverently interpreted and taught thusly. Creation and development of Earth's landscape and biota were about global upheavals that coincided with major depositional gaps in the succession of strata of certain regions of Europe, such as the well-studied Paris Basin. This doctrine came to be called Catastrophism, because of its reliance on global cataclysms to account for the complex geology and biology of a very young Earth as proven by Biblical scripture.

In the late 18th century, the Scotsman James Hutton came to an entirely different realization. He suspected that slow, day-to-day processes like erosion, transport, and deposition by a river, could level alpine mountains and fill in broad basins, provided that they operated over long intervals of deep time. This principle dubbed Uniformitarianism flew in the face of Catastrophism, because it postulated that slow, systematic processes were the principal, if not sole, agents of geologic change on Earth. Hence, the planet's ancient past, according to Uniformitarianists, must be deep and long – involving hundreds of millions rather than mere thousands of years – and could be understood without recourse to supernatural causes.

This "anti-religionist" philosophy provided the thematic fiber for the three volume set of *Principles of Geology*, published by the Englishman Charles Lyell in the early 1830s. These seminal books gave credence to Hutton's Uniformitarianism, the anti-Catastrophist doctrine that the geologic past was expansive and consisted of natural events interpretable by supposing that "the present is the key to the past." This original book greatly influenced the thinking of Charles Darwin who took a copy of

Lyell's first volume with him to sea, where he served as the ship-captain's conversationalist and eventually as naturalist aboard the *HMS Beagle*.

As it turned out, one of the major objections to Darwin's theory of biological evolution by natural selection was the need for an ancient Earth. The thermodynamic calculations of eminent physicists of the time, particularly those of Lord Kelvin, indicated decidedly that Earth had been fit for habitation by plants and animals for no more than a hundred million years and likely for much less than that. These numerical computations based on the latest physical theories of energy and matter caused Darwin such anguish that he modified and even retracted some of his more controversial inferences about rates of evolutionary change in later editions of his influential book *On the Origin of Species*.

Since that time, observations, measurements, and particularly the radioactive dating of rocks have indubitably established the multi-billion-year legacy of Earth, allowing Uniformitarianism and evolutionary biology to flourish throughout the 20th century.

Geologists of today carry on the Uniformitarianist's tradition of Hutton and Lyell. Consequently, explanations of natural phenomena grounded in catastrophe are abhorrent, because such notions provide dangerous support to the discredited ideas of modern Creationists, who continue resolutely to propound that Earth and all of its inhabitants are a recent creation of a Christian God.

Despite this real concern, Ted prods his geologic critics "to throw out the books and papers on the systematic geomorphic evolution of the southern coast of New South Wales, and look at the field evidence and believe your own eyes." He does not demur to the reproof of his detractors and defends the interpretation of what he sees with zeal and eloquence. The Late Quaternary development of these shores, he insists resolutely, is about catastrophe, about widespread and random devastation by large walls of water. This coastline is not about a uniform, step-by-slow-step progression of landform development, whereby bits of bedrock are slowly ground into sand by surf breakers to form beaches. This is heavyweight brutality, not interminable jabbing, but rather a knockout punch delivered by Mohammed Ali. Tsunamis kayoed the shore, Ted insists. Bam and in the blink of an eye the mismatch was over. Notwithstanding Aesop's wisdom, here in coastal New South Wales, the hare does beat out the tortoise.

What exactly happens when a tsunami engulfs a headland? Such a query animates Ted, as he attempts with words and gestures to familiarize us with the fierceness of this short-lived process. Drawing from the eyewitness accounts of historical tsunamis and using equations that relate the erosional power to the height of a tsunami, the depth of water flow, the size of entrained boulders, and the scale of bedforms, Ted stirs the imagination of his listeners.

"What's out of the ordinary about the tsunamis that struck this segment of Australia's shoreline," he begins "is the direction they approached the coast." Judging from the alignment of imbricated boulders and the position of dump deposits, these enormous waves appear to have come out of the southeast and northeast quadrants. This means that the crest of the tsunami did not face the coast like an incoming ocean swell, but was oriented near perpendicular to it and thus traveled along the shore, progressively overwashing a series of half-a-kilometer-long bedrock headlands. In essence, these were flank assaults and the brunt of the collapsing wall of water struck the sides rather than the seaward points of the rock promontories.

The collapsing wave planed the tops of headlands and plastered them with smear deposits of gravel, sand, and mud. The rocky headland points were sheared off and reduced to hummocky, keeled, or planed platforms, depending on the local hydrodynamic conditions and the durability of the bedrock. After overtopping a rock promontory, the wave traveled across the embayment located on the lee side of the headland and struck the opposite shore, carving rock cusps into its sea cliffs. Wave run-up deposited sand, gravel, and cobbles as far as half-a-kilometer inland. This progression of events was repeated at each headland as the wave traveled north or south along the regional trend of the coastline, systematically bashing into and over each promontory and spreading out across the intervening embayments.

According to Ted, there are other aspects of a tsunami's flow dynamics that few people appreciate. They involve the incredible erosive power of high-velocity fluid flow, particularly in water that is no more than several meters deep. Under this hydrodynamic condition, tiny unstable bubbles spontaneously appear in the water and immediately burst, releasing a powerful hydraulic force that remarkably can punch holes into hard rock. This cavitation process produces a variety of small shock structures on rock terraces high above the level of high tide, such as star-shaped impact marks, drill holes, V-shaped grooves, and potholes. The rapid flow of water can also create powerful lift forces that pluck large slabs of rock off platforms and move them tens and even hundreds of meters. This assertion is supported by more than mere theoretical argument. On March 27, 1964, Good Friday, a large tsunami slammed into the Alaska Railway terminal at Seward in Prince William Sound, Alaska. Unbelievably, heavy locomotives were lifted by the wall of water and carried as water-borne projectiles for as far as fifty meters.

When a tsunami washes over a promontory, the surge of water accelerates as it becomes constricted by the topographic obstruction. As a result, vortices, which can be likened to tornadoes in unstable air, form in the high-speed, turbulent water. Once created, these funnels of water can grow in breadth and length, spin faster and faster, and cavitate the solid rock. If contact at one spot of the ground is prolonged, the vortex sculpts a large circular crater, termed a whirlpool, into the bedrock.

Ted showed us examples of these erosional features, which are well exposed on basalt surfaces that crop out along the outer reaches of Bass Point. When you stare into them, they look like miniature open-pit mines with one notable exception: a bedrock mound occupies their centers. According to Ted, the strong rotational speeds at the periphery of the water funnel cut deeply into the rock and excavate a circular pit with an outside edge of cavitated, step-shaped rock. Because the rotational flow velocities decrease towards the center of the vortex, less bedrock is eroded there, accounting for the central mound of the whirlpool. The high-speed spin of vortices apparently can sculpt other landform features as well. Ted believes that their erosive power hollowed out the many sea caves and sea arches of New South Wales, and wherever bedrock was highly fractured blew out tunnels, like the Blowhole of Kiama and the Gosangs Tunnel of Jervis Bay.

There we have it, the tsunami – a genuine, geologic catastrophe of Herculean dimensions unrecognized as a legitimate agent of geomorphic change. Most geologists understand the evolution of the southern coast of New South Wales to involve centuries, even millennia, of slow and acceptable abrasion of bedrock by ocean swell accentuated by the agreeable up-and-down gestures of the tide. This conceptualization of shoreline development, which is taught and applied everywhere in the world, complies with the traditional precepts of the Uniformitarianist doctrine.

The problem, Ted asserts, is that it flies in the face of the field evidence in certain coastal sectors. Here along the vast southeastern seaboard of New South Wales, he insists, many of the landforms and shoreline deposits are not painstakingly crafted at a snail's pace by ocean waves and tides, but are the result of mere hours of pernicious destruction. A sky-high wall of wild water, roiling with vortices, spinning out of control, and chock-full of debris, is what battered senseless this strip of coast and changed its seascape evermore. What was left behind by the furious, hours-long assault of a tsunami was a devastated landscape of decapitated headlands and broken rock that boldly overprints the signature of the prevailing day-to-day effects of ocean swell. If this account is correct, and remember that most coastal geologists regard it as problematical, some even farcical, this is truly a momentous "turning against," and tsunamis would rank high on everyone's favorite list of honest-to-goodness natural catastrophes.

But there's more horror associated with this cataclysmic activity. Humans living in New South Wales may actually have witnessed the destruction of their land by one of these towering tsunamis. As summarized in Ted's book, Aboriginal people belonging to the Burragorang clan recall in legend a time long ago when both the sky and the ocean fell down on their ancestors.

The tale begins at the end of a fiery, hot day. Mercifully, the sun had finally set. In the cool stillness of the early evening and without warning, the world abruptly became unhinged. People stared, paralyzed with fear, as the moon and the stars crumbled and then broke apart. The sky caught fire as burning chunks of stars fell to the ground and smoldered everywhere. Unbelievably, the night's terror worsened. Suddenly, a huge ball of blue flame, hissing and burning, turned the night into day and with explosive force slammed hard into the ground, splitting it wide open. The people cowered together, fearful for their lives, as burning bits of stars and heavy rain fell on them throughout the long night.

The next morning, they discovered huge, smoke-darkened holes all over their land. To their astonishment, new caves were cut into the sea cliffs. Later, neighboring tribes told them that the ocean as well as the stars had fallen in. During that momentous night inscribed in the deep memory of these Aboriginal people, the entire universe had come crashing down, and so fire, rain, and ocean water had fallen on them, burning and flooding the land, killing many people.

This traditional story has an explicit meaning for Ted. What else could it signify, but the frenzied exploits of a tsunami? On that fateful night, a meteorite likely flared through the sky and exploded on impact with the ocean, vaporizing in a flash millions of tons of seawater. This vapor condensed throughout the night and fell as heavy downpours. The torrential rain abruptly soaked the ground and flooded all the streams and rivers of the region.

Meanwhile, a tsunami or more likely a series of tsunamis generated by the meteorite's explosive blow, radiated outward from the impact point and traveled rapidly towards the land like a ring of wavelets raised by a pebble tossed into a puddle of water. Offshore, the tsunami's crests lay flat and unimposing, conserving their strength for later. Once in sight of land, they grew serious. The waves deliberately slowed in the shallow water, garnered all of their might, and reached up for the stars.

Aboriginal people – wet, cold, and terrified – would have been unaware of the impending madness because of the night's inky darkness and drenching rain. Those huddled in rock shelters along the shore likely heard a hissing sound, looked up to the sky, and during the last moment of their lives saw a colossal wall of raging water high above them come crashing down. The end was mercifully quick for most of them. The inland survivors were traumatized for all time, and a legend was born and burnt into the conscious memory of their descendants.

Ted believes that this Aboriginal myth is grounded in factual reality, because it explains a number of anthropological discoveries in the region. To begin, the widespread devastation associated with a tsunami battering the coastal land at that time patently accounts for dump deposits found at the head of some bays. Interestingly, mixed in some of their chaotic rubble is a profusion of exquisite Aboriginal hand axes and hand-hewed blades. These likely came from Aboriginal camps on nearby headlands that were overtopped by the giant waves, their surge sweeping away these tools and plastering them with mud and gravel against the head of the adjoining embayment as high as ten meters above the normal level of the sea.

Furthermore, the tsunami storyline makes intelligible some aberrant changes in the living habits of coastal people that occurred at about the time of the alleged tsunami disaster. Take the case of coastal middens younger than 500 years old. These do not contain seashell litter, the dominant refuse material of the more ancient coastal middens. What could have caused this sudden and exceptional dietary change? As claimed by Ted, it's explained by the collapse of the marine, hard-ground habitats of inshore waters. The tsunami simply scraped all the shellfish beds off the rock platforms so that this traditional food resource, abundant before the devastation of that grim-faced night, was no longer available. In order to avert starvation, coastal people had little choice but to hunt finfish instead of gathering shellfish.

Coincidentally, rock shelters well inland of the shore began to be used heavily about that time. This demographic shift has traditionally been understood as a natural reaction to the pressure of a burgeoning coastal population. Ted believes otherwise. He suggests that it more likely reflects the abandonment of shore camps by coastal clans out of a deep fear that the ocean might once again fall out of the eastern sky. Interestingly, this version is consistent with the observations of the earliest European explorers of the region, who were perplexed by the fact that Aboriginal people seemed to avoid living along the coast, despite the glorious, tranquil settings, the refreshing sea breezes, and the abundance of seafood.

Given the descriptions and arguments above, it seems to be as certain as anything can be in geology that tsunamis have by and large influenced, if not out-and-out directed, the development of the shore's landscape along southern New South Wales. But feelings and opinions in the practice of science matter a great deal regardless of claims to the contrary.

The majority of geologists look askance at Ted's tsunami proposal, his most ardent critics regarding it as heretical, the product of an audacious misrepresentation of facts, at the very least a barefaced misreading of landforms. They have confidence in the time-tested conventional models of coastal evolution, which rely on the steady erosion of headlands by wind-generated, storm waves and the formation of beach deposits by the longshore drift of sand. This point is emphasized by the fact that the textbooks commonly used in many university courses that I inspected – one dealing with coastal evolution, another with coastal geomorphology, and a third with coastal systems – do not even mention the word tsunami, never mind treat it as a legitimate geomorphic concept applicable to coastal landform evolution.

Ted's detractors agree that tsunamis exist and that they unquestionably strike shorelines. But in their view, they are exceptional occurrences and have no lasting effect on the deposits and contours of the seaside. Whatever the devastation of coastal land by giant waves, regardless of its scale, it is outdone by the incessant wearing down of rock and piling up of sand by shore breakers.

Ted does not balk. They are blatantly wrong, he claims. And he has since found evidence of ancient tsunami-generated landscapes and deposits in other places in Australia, including the northeast coast of Queensland and the northwest coast of West Australia, and suspects they're elsewhere in the world, notably in Chile, Scotland, Norway, Hawaii, the Bahamas, and the Canary Islands. Recently, other researchers have published scientific papers making similar claims for the shoreline surrounding the North Sea.

In all fairness, the skeptics do have reproof regarding some aspects of Ted's tsunami hypothesis. Huge boulders, for example, are displaced shoreward by large breakers during storms. Hence, there is no need to call upon a tsunami to explain their repositioning. Also, ocean swell undergo wave refraction in shallow water, a process that focuses wave energy at bedrock promontories and promotes the formation of sea caves wherever the rock is weakened by fractures. Over time, the caves are widened and deepened. With prolonged wave attack, some evolve into tunnels and then into sea arches. Eventually, the rock bridges are undermined and collapse into rubble, with only a cluster of irregular sea stacks remaining upright.

Given this well documented process, it seems preposterous to claim that the morphology of sea caves is the result of tsunami destruction. What is more, some of the features in basalts, such as whirlpools, construed to be drilled-out structures created by tsunami vortices may merely be the result of swelling and cracking of the thin crust of lava flows as they cooled. Hence, most geologists interpret them as primary volcanic structures rather than tsunami impact features.

Who is right? Who is wrong? How is truth established or falsehood revealed? Such queries have engaged the human intellect for millennia. Going as far back as 400 B.C., Socrates argued that the correctness of any idea is independent of either its popularity or its vilification. Nor, he insisted, is it contingent upon whether a majority of people considers a belief to be genuine or erroneous. The measure of truthfulness, Socrates maintained, is determined solely by rational examination of the evidence and the logical cogency of the argument, including the reasonableness of its underlying assumptions.

Where did this insight lead Socrates? Notwithstanding his sound, clear-headed thinking, the will of the majority overrode his sagacity. A jury of his contemporaries in a court of law condemned Socrates to death for his commonsensical conviction that logical reason alone can reveal truth independent of authority.

As taught and practiced by Socrates, the natural sciences likewise endeavor to distinguish truth from falsehood by the directive of reason. But proof in the sciences, unlike in the abstract domain of mathematics, is frustratingly elusive. In fact, absolute proof is theoretically impossible to achieve in the practice of science. A well-designed experiment can disprove a long held belief, if the experimental findings are at variance with the theory's dictates. What few appreciate, however, is that close, even exact, agreement between the prediction of a hypothesis and the outcome of an experiment or a field survey is not a categorical measure of proof. Rather, the logical conclusion derived from such investigations is that their results did not falsify the hypothesis. If repeated attempts to refute the postulation fail to do so, then the hypothesis may be upgraded to a theory, which signifies that it is considered to be a cogent, legitimate, and useful approximation of reality, but not an absolute truth. After all, it could still be disproven by later scientific findings.

This intellectualization may be all well and good. But how exactly does it help us resolve the scientific dispute between the dissenting viewpoint of Ted Bryant and the authoritative conventionalism of most coastal geologists? After all, these two fundamentally different visualizations of shoreline evolution of southern New South Wales cannot be equally correct, although either or both of the representations could certainly be false.

The question left hanging, however, revolves around a quandary, some would argue an impossibility, of experimentally testing hypotheses that interpret events long past. Unlike physics and chemistry, the disciplines of geology, paleontology, evolutionary biology, and astronomy have a strong historical context. Nobody actually witnessed the formation of Earth and its landscapes, the genesis of species, and the creation of the universe. Historically based sciences must rely on accurate observations and logical inferences about the aftermath – rocks, species, stars – of bygone occurrences, relying on the centricity of Uniformitarianism to unearth the nature and sequence of the processes that produced these effects. The inability to conceive, design, and execute the discerning experiment explains why controversies among geologists, evolutionary biologists, and cosmologists are pervasive and endure for a very long time before the collective wisdom of the contenders can resolve the dispute to the satisfaction of most.

A gut instinct about the tsunami controversy tells me that truth is located in the entangled middle ground between the two extreme points of view. What is fundamental to one extreme perspective is peripheral to the other and vice versa. My hunch is that along the seaside of New South Wales the routine operations of headland erosion by waves and sand deposition by currents prevailed, until the power of a cataclysmic tsunami demolished in an instant hundreds and even thousands of years of effort to fashion methodically the region's coastal landscape.

The aftermath of a tsunami battering is literally a "turning against" Uniformitarianism, and is therefore deserving of the epithet "catastrophe." My sense is that this combined pair of competing ideas – one underscoring continuity and systematic development, the other stressing discontinuity and cataclysmic change – provides the symmetry necessary for explaining the world. After all, the very essence of each of our life's experience is the continual interplay of harmony and dissonance, complacency and tragedy, is it not?

What is truly fascinating about this clash of ideas is not the controversy *per se*, but what it discloses about our subconscious aversion to a mortal existence in a natural world replete with chaotic rumblings. Most people loathe the arbitrary fickleness of the natural human condition. In an effort to thwart these apprehensions, we have created a technical world of artifact, in which control and prediction are prescribed. We technological modernists are prideful, even boastful, of our ingenuity at adapting the wilderness to our needs and desires, even proclaiming triumphantly that we have extricated ourselves from the humdrum messiness of natural forces to the point that *Homo sapiens* is no longer subject to the evolutionary pressures of natural selection.

Our predilection for a manufactured world of tidiness, continuity, orderliness, and reliability fosters the comforting expectation that tomorrow will be much like today. And what is driven out of our consciousness is that Nature's spectacles – its volcanoes, ice caps, meteorite impacts, mass extinctions, earthquakes, landslides, droughts, hurricanes, climate change, and yes tsunamis – are at the very core of the human predicament and will ultimately determine our destiny, as they always have and always will for all species. How can it be otherwise?

In the human world, it is the self-righteous conviction of our preeminence that makes us resist enfolding a truly catastrophic process into our scientific models of natural environments. Shoreline evolution, a case in point, is conceived as a single set of deterministic, linear, and cause-and-effect interactions, largely powered by the day-to-day assault of the land by ocean swell.

Imagining coastal landforms as developing in this gradual, systematic, and predictable way is immensely reassuring, because the forces of change are continuous and thus foreseeable and lie well within the bounds of human manipulation. As such, we can with confidence control or at the very least mitigate the slow wearing away of the coast by engineering solutions such as seawalls, riprap, groins, jetties, and breakwaters.

Yet this is delusional, because it denies the existence of discontinuous forces mightier than human yearnings. According to Ted Bryant, a tsunami will once again wash over the seaboard of New South Wales. Although the precise timing, place, and magnitude of this event cannot be known, there is no doubt whatsoever of its inevitability. Because of our false sense of supremacy and the large and growing populations of coastal cities and towns, it will be a dreadfully catastrophic occurrence involving a tremendous loss of both life and property that few are emotionally and psychologically prepared to handle.

Lest we forget, the natural world is inherently chaotic and catastrophic, and we are powerless to make it be otherwise for the long term despite claims to the contrary. Each dawn, everyone expects the new day to be much like the day before. There is a dangerous innocence in the expectation that the future can be emptied of its fatal possibilities. That is not the nature of Nature as the ancient rock record clearly demonstrates.

PART II
The Nature of Deep Time

DEEP TIME'S STONEWORK

"There was some wisdom, it seemed, in coming to terms with the fact that there could be something beyond what felt like nothing. That there were realities outside of imagination."

Jennifer du Bois, 2012, *A Partial History of Lost Causes*

One early June morning, shivering in thigh-deep snow, I am staring at the gunmetal gray face of a cliff. I am belaying my partner who is struggling above me to twist a screw into a slab of ice for protection. A thousand feet below me, a glacier creeps at a geologic pace and, unlike us, is sensibly going downhill. Its glassy surface, lumpy and scree-dirtied, is crisscrossed with fractures, as if the massive ice had lost its grip of the cirque wall and smashed to the ground. I shiver and go inward, feeling unfamiliar shifts in my body and mind.

Suddenly I notice thin beds of shale gorged with tiny clamshells just centimeters from my face. These fossils have been at high altitude forever. Then it penetrates. We're climbing an uplifted seabed. The space now filled with the weight of this mountainside was once an expanse of ocean before its gray mud hardened into stone. The sedimentary beds were crushed and pushed skyward during a mountain-building orogeny that occurred several hundred million years ago. How can we make sense of such tectonic events, of such interminable eons shoved forever into Earth's geologic past? What will hang here in place of this mountainside on some fresh morning of Earth's deep future? Given the transience of the natural world, how can the flesh and blood of our lived moments mean anything?

How is it possible to reconcile the tension between the brevity of human life with the vastness of deep time?

Let's begin with a fact: the age of Earth is calculated to be about 4.6 billion-years old. This measurement claims that a particular event in Earth's history – its beginning – has slipped into the past and is now some 4.6 billion years 'behind' the 21st century. This conclusion seems straightforward, but it's not.

A closer reading reveals that not one, but two histories are wrapped into the statement that Earth is 4.6 billion years old. First, there is the epochal event itself, the creation of the planet, which is done with. And then there is the long history of that discrete event, meaning that Earth's genesis once was 'situated' in the immediate present and now has 'vanished' into the far past. As Arthur Prior argues in *Papers on Time and Tense*, "(t)here is....the difficulty that we generally think of the history of a thing as the sum of what it does and what happens to it *while it is there* – when it ceases to be, its history has ended – and this does make it seem odd that there should be an indefinitely long history of something which itself occupies a time which is indefinitely short." Prior's perspective distinguishes "between the history that an event *has*, and the bit of history that it *is*." Put simply, it *is* and that is its bit of history; it *was* and that is its long history.

This realization reveals how the current millennium gets woven into the fabric of the geologic past. Landscapes, poised at the edge of chaos, maintain themselves by untiring self-organization, impacted by countless, unrelenting contingencies. Once emergent, however, the newness of a landscape, whatever and wherever it is, is transient. As time passes and its surroundings change across different temporal and spatial scales, landscapes maintain themselves tenaciously until they cannot, and then they are no more. Steadfastness is anomalous, impermanence habitual. Existence, whether granitic or organic, is all about vanishing into oblivion.

Nature has no philosophy, no theology, no direction, no concerns; people do. Earth has no preferred state of existence; it becomes whatever it becomes, always poised between order and disorder. In such a chaotic world going nowhere in particular, nothing is certain except unintended changes, unremitting disturbances, and numerous phase transitions. Constancy is what humans crave, flux is all that there is.

There are undertones within deep time, derivable from the inborn condition of Nature as a complex adaptive system. The far past is not shriveled up and done with as we suppose; it continues to accrue an unbroken history. The present is its turbulent wake as the future suddenly emerges and then brusquely surges into the past. Because the past is time gone by and the future is time yet to be, the lived vibrancy of the material world exists only and firmly in the matrix of the ever-present moments.

As the physicist Lawrence W. Fagg penned in *The Becoming of Time*: "Moments, moments, moments, notes in the symphony of time." This mellifluous 'flow' has streamed uninterrupted for billions of years, day-by-day improvisations that created Earth's history, including the flickering into life of inanimate material. Earth's 4.6-billion-year legacy is the wake of the everlasting now – an immutable present that has endured since the beginning of time.

Without a present, there is no time, a view shared by many human cultures. Robert Heilbroner in *Visions of the Future: The Distant Past, Yesterday, Today, and Tomorrow* writes: "In a manner of speaking, there is neither future nor past in prehistoric societies. There is only an immense present, stretching backward and forward like an ever-changing but always unchanged veld, jungle, ocean, sky." Put simply, tomorrow is yesterday.

But truly, what to make of a seabed and its load of clamshells shoved upward into the sky and now crumbling into rubble in the glowing warmth of the sun that will one day become feverish and then go stone-cold dead? Why risk life ascending the stillness of a towering ridge of rock-hard seafloor? Is human existence fated to be yet another small delirium in Earth's wild past?

The musings of most people about such matters are mostly self-justified and self-aggrandized. Unfortunately, sophism – the act of deceptive, self-serving argument – is often confounded with rationalism. What we do know is that multiple possible outcomes, uncertain and unintentional as they are, confront the chaotic emergence of landscapes. Only one of those many possible futures will materialize into the moments of a day, which then will accrete to the topside of the deep past. As the historian John Lewis Gaddis in *The Landscape of History* puts it, "…. continuities intersect contingencies, contingencies encounter continuities, and through this process history is made."

Like all species, *Homo sapiens* emerged out of a long evolutionary narrative of crises conscripted by natural selection. As such, Earth's materiality, dimly perceived and understood though it is, lays claim to the happenstance of *Homo sapiens*, making human life and its fate as tangible as a lithified seabed of fossil clams weathering out of a mountainside and plummeting into the abyss of deep time.

From this evolutionary perspective, it follows that humans have external and internal fastenings to Earth. Although our flesh and senses react without thought to immediate stimuli, the genetic makeup of our cells, passed down to each of us from the first shiver of life, knows about deep history, about light and darkness long gone.

The ecologist Michael Soule stresses this very point in David Takacs' *The Idea of Biodiversity: Philosophies of Paradise*. He says: "....but – speaking as a scientist – our genetic material remembers the days in the organic soup when we were simply a few biochemical pathways – they're still there. They haven't changed hardly at all from the bacterial days." And so, inscriptions of secrets tucked away in cellular DNA, oceans of genetic memory inscribed as a molecular code, connect us to Earth's faraway past. The whispers of Cro-Magnon people are in our genes as well as the heat of the Precambrian sun. Otherwise, *Homo sapiens* could not have become.

It should now be apparent why the radioactive dating of bedrock, no matter how exhilarating and audacious, is not enough to manifest the lyric verses of deep time – its ageless rhythms and asymmetries, its stillness and contingencies, its refrains and marginalia, its ice fields and deserts. Earth's age is an outlier of something far more expansive and fertile than quantity, in the same way that a life is far grander than the dullness of a person's age. The rich geologic narratives that fill the bedrock anatomy of landscapes show this to be true.

Deep time abstracted to numbers and shorn of circumstances is denied its reality, because, as Ann Spirn claims in *The Language of Landscape*, "...they are not the things they describe, but always one or more steps removed." The point then is to sideslip into wildness, seeking to sense the world from within the shadow forms that are subsumed by the crudeness of facts. I realized finally that the quest for understanding our authentic humanism must be wider, higher, and deeper than strange facts remembered and odd stones collected. And so, I sought to become a time-traveler of deep time.

All well and good, but how can expansive time be experienced given how quickly the years slip away into the past? Does sensing the eminence of the deep past require another side to our lives? Should we draw back or darken the shadows of daybreak and twilight? Is deep time about wonder or reason, stillness or restlessness, or something else entirely? At long last an approach to get beyond these confounding thoughts occurred to me. Somehow, I must locate myself in deep time. But where exactly is deep time today?

Recall that the deep past accretes moment by moment from the everlasting present, the long now that always changes and never ends. Obviously this implies that deep time is everywhere today. How could it be otherwise, because the present is all that there ever is. No lacuna separates Earth's creation from its still-accreting, long geo-evolutionary history. And yet poised at this active edge that is today, why are we so insensible to deep time's comportment? We wake up, realize that it's the morning of a new day, and go about our business. This is the problem. The infinitely small details of our bustling lives obscure the infinitely quiet reach of the long now. It is this narrowly focused way of inhabiting our human-built world that prevents our sensing the moments that are always accreting to Earth's 4.6-billion-year past.

Imagine the heap of slow-moving days that were needed to transform a wet seabed full of seashells into the bedrock shoulder of a mountainside. Meanwhile, the DNA molecules of the first life forms that emerged some 3.8 billion years ago have been passed on to posterity and one day are biologically expressed as a mountaineer clambering up the ridgeline of a lithified seabed.

How to make sense of such complex interrelatedness that squirms its way blindly into tomorrow? How can we know what the solid stones know? We are not gods; we are an animal species, *Homo sapiens*, limited and yet enriched by the earthiness of both our lifeblood and wistful imagination. Some events we understand at once; others we understand slowly or not at all.

We might well begin our search for deep time by asking where on Earth is a deep past apparent. Certainly, it is not found in the hubbub of cityscapes where clocked time flourishes, though the deep past gathers into its clutch city days alongside forest days. Nor on farms, pastures, and gardens where land is subjugated to plant and animal domestication. In such places, thoughts about daily weather and seasonal harvests are clotted together in the foreground, obscuring the massive backdrop of the everlasting present.

Most surprisingly, deep time is not necessarily conspicuous even in wilderness. Consider the steamy tropics of Amazonia. There, vast tracts of thick rainforest are overfilled with diverse, fast-growing trees and bewildering communities of organisms, a thriving intimacy beyond compare. And it is this exuberant ecology that detracts us from sensing the slow-paced time over which the rainforest lives all of its days. Such a profusion of growth is mostly sustained by rapid decay and brisk uptake of nutrients, ecological processes imprinted on the stillness of everlasting time that binds ecosystems to Earth's deep past.

It turns out that the resplendency of the long past is affirmed mostly in open, barren landscapes such as mountains with their messy spines of broken stone. The high ground of Earth, as Anne Spirn describes insightfully in *The Language of Landscape*, "emerge(d) out of ancient, ongoing violence and inexorable, eternal erosion." There, the murmurs of stones evoke memories of worlds long vanquished but still enduring. As few can, William Faulkner enriches the meaning of this crucial point in *Requiem for a Nun* with this thundering utterance: "The past is never dead. It's not even past."

All well and good, but given that the human world is framed wholly by words and symbols, how exactly do we access the mute rocks of landscapes except as an abstract quantity? One way is to accept the subjective truth of individual sensations, the realm of inward existence explored so thoroughly by Soren Keirkegaard. He argues that personal truths are not about reason, nor about the objective findings of science. Rather they emerge from inside individuals who commit to a long, contemplative life that allows passionate, sensuous feelings to infuse their consciousness. As Kierkegaard argues, subjective truths disclose authentic insights into the inward, unique being each of us is.

This perspective resonates with the findings of the Danish psychiatrist Joost Meerloo who proclaims in J. T. Fraser's book *The Voices of Time* that each of us is "an ambassador of (our) instinctual archaic needs" that are biologically inherited through the self-organized history of evolution. Meerloo is convinced that an individual perception of living beyond time manifests itself from "an actual experience triggering off an unconscious memory without the memory being conscious." This may explain how occasional tight-fisted stirrings, ancient echoes of echoes buried in the tangled chemistry of our DNA, suddenly angle out into our conscious mind when surrounded by the fractured rawness of rock-ribbed crags.

The pregnant insights of subjective truth, I've come to believe, are authentic portals for re-imagining the distant past. Inside of us are unconscious DNA couplings rooted deeply to everything underfoot. One doesn't have to understand deep time in order to feel its essence. One simply inhabits the crevices of unscripted stone alone, quiet and receptive to the settlings of Earth's incessant present.

When drawn to the fierce cliffs of high mountains, internal feelings resonate with ancient stonework and thicken one's imagination. Divining wonder and dread at being genuinely alive among wild stones, the mind glimpses dark shadings of the past far too big for words and numbers, expanses of time when pooled seas dried up and hardened into summit ridgelines. The sharp and rounded edges of rocks, their textures and patterns, their cracked surfaces streaked by rain and lichen, reflect the chaos of the tumultuous whole that is the reality of today.

This manner of 'sensing,' of opening oneself up to the quiet rhythms of rock exposures, jumps the mind into the fullness of deep time, "like skies seen in water," as the poet William Stanley Merwin imagined it. Once accessed, the powerful memories of such seamless encounters with time never lie still.

I remember well the stern silence that filled a restless day of my life. I was alone somewhere in the Dry Valleys of Antarctica, trudging up a messy, windless hollow void of sound. Stepped cliffs of sandstone separated the blaze of the sky from the cold rubble of the valley. The day frozen to the boulder-strewn ground lacked contour. Bewildered, I kept glancing back at the glacial dirt over which I had trod, unaware that I was slowly becoming a creature of time more than of place. Abruptly, a headwall loomed in front of me, its stillness immense despite the soundless day. Layer-upon-layer of sandstone stacked up quietly to the sky, piles of boundless history wasting away in cold sunshine.

Disquieted by the solitude, I stared long and hard at the crags and hollows of the landform. Where am I? Something loose was stirring deep inside of me, dimly perceived. Suddenly, it avalanched into feelings of overwhelming endlessness far beyond the ordinariness of time, not out there but from deep inside my body. At that moment, I had come to be the self-effacing human described by Erazin Kohak in *The Embers and the Stars*, "who, living at the intersection of time and eternity, can bring the eternal into time – and raise time to eternity." Old roots from within my body entered the ground, the cold stones adding depth and mass to my primal self.

Later that day, I encountered the gutted base of a headwall. I began to climb with difficulty, breathing heavily. It was cold and still. I was clinging precariously to stiff beds of sandstone scraped raw by glaciers and wind. Their grains of sand were organized into intricate ripples and crossbeds, like the lilt of poems. Above them were gray siltstones and green mudstones grimy with fossilized leaf litter. A sharp-edged, coal seam, black as night, ended the sequence. All these sedimentary patterns represent a still life of the deep past, inserted into the immediate, dynamic moments of today.

I look down at the sandstone at my feet and unexpectedly feel the pull of the ancient river's flow. Its swift, tumbling currents form eddies and standing waves that rip up sand from the channel bottom. A few trees along a cutbank are uprooted and dragged along by the tumbling rush of water. A silicified log in the sandstone by my feet shows annual growth rings, having lived fourteen years leaning towards the river before it fell and drowned.

For centuries, possibly millennia, the languid run of the river sculpted point bars arranged as festooned beds of fine-grained sand, stacked one atop the other. Meanwhile, tight meander loops of the river channel pinched off and became isolated oxbow lakes. These quarter-moon basins filled in with silt and mud darkened by leaf litter from copses of trees rooted to the lakeshore. In places, peat built up, wherever marsh plants and bog trees overgrew pools of standing water. One day, tens of millions of years into the future, the sedimentary sequence was buried and the peat was transformed to anthracite by the extreme pressure of the thick overburden.

The refrain – sandstone, siltstone, mudstone, coalstone – repeats itself over and over upward into the massive brow of the headwall and sings me out. I touch the stone tribute of this long-vanished floodplain. I am clumsy with cold and yet my feelings are deeply warmed by this encounter with Antarctica's faraway past that remains lodged into the long now of today.

Back at base camp, buried in two down sleeping bags, I'm warm and exhausted, yet cannot sleep. Wind gusts continually slap the tent. What just happened to me in that scoured valley? This strange, sidelong encounter with Nature was powerful and disturbing. Solitude and fatigue had evidently unfurled my thoughts. Somehow the lay of the land pressed in, causing remembrances from long ago to rear up from within my being, ghostly fluvial meanderings across an ancient floodplain, now costumed as beds of stone. Old stories enter "the bog in our brains and bowels," as Henry David Thoreau quipped. Years later, I described this occurrence to a friend. He listened intently and said: "It was a radical seeing of the world, of yourself as part of it. You were eclipsed and so became whole."

Since then, I've had many such experiences usually while mountaineering, always when alone and settled into a stark, stony backland. Being *of* Nature and not simply *in* Nature, encountering one's evolutionary self in the heft of deep time, involves feeling the all-encompassing grandeur of the natural world. It entails being quiet, not speaking but listening, and enduring the sublime stillness of fractured bedrock. It is a reversal of the intellectual being that I was raised to be, a deportment that, according to David Oates in *Paradise Wild*, leads to a "resistant cultural layer, the fundamentalist/literalist stratum that wants a flat, one-reading world."

Distancing oneself from pure Kantian reason enraptures the mind, releasing the wonder and dread of subtle, yet complex, memories of bedrock that paradoxically loop back on the self, which in turn humanizes the stone. At such moments, the self and Earth become entirely one. In some comforting way, this ontology of sensing the present as timeless, of actuating the breath of wildness deep inside, authenticates my creaturely existence and provides a welcoming home for my ecological afterlife.

The exterior stonework of landscapes is what we see and know. Their internal qualities – the hidden depths of enormous volumes of time – are what elude us. The rational laws of physics and chemistry, the faith-based accounts of religion, the dreamy aesthetics of art, all of them ingenious affirmations of the human heart and mind, are mere surface reflections of the enormous weight of countless moments collapsed into beds of stone and into the script of our DNA molecules.

What exactly is time? We don't know, as confirmed by the vast philosophical and scientific literature about the deportment of time. At best we rely on metaphors to conceptualize time's essence: time flows, time unfolds, time's arrow, the sands of time, the shadow cast by the sun, the axial spin of Earth, the tick of the clock, the delta t of calculus. But as Henry Wadsworth Longfellow surmised, "....these are but arbitrary and outward signs, the measures of Time, not Time itself."

Some argue that because we measure time, it exists. But as Robert Lanza points out in *A New Theory of the Universe*, "Einstein sidestepped th(is) question by simply defining time as "what we measure with a clock.""" Even the phrase 'deep' time relies on spatial characterization. The sea is deep, but time as deepness makes no sense, if one thinks critically about it. As George Lakoff and Mark Johnson describe in *Philosophy in the Flesh*, time is "conceptualized as locations on a landscape." As evidence, they list "locational expressions (that) have temporal correlates: long, short, extend, spread, over, on, runs, from, to come, close to, within, in, at, pass, through, reach, and down the road." Time in and of itself seemingly cannot be known, because metaphors are not truths but obliging comparisons, and so understanding time's nature must necessarily be oblique. Time is itself and so what to do?

Well time, whatever it may be, does not stand apart from the whole that is Nature. I believe that time is not simply a discrete fourth dimension, nor is it an absolute measure of anything. Rather it is the animated aspect of a world richly textured by the emergent processes and patterns of self-organized landscapes. Time is impossible without change and change is impossible without time; the two are inseparable.

Given that geological, evolutionary, and ecological transformations are complex, it follows that time likewise must be multi-layered and organic, much more than a count of elapsed years, no matter its expansiveness. The radioactive dating of rock under-appreciates this point. Absolute-age dating imposes a simple numerical chronology on the milestones of the deep past, which reifies Earth's dynamism, its patterns and processes, into objects of history conflated into a linear, geologic time scale.

The marvel of learning that a body of granite is some millions or billions of years old overshadows its wonderfully complex history that continues to accrete, because it is still part of an evolving landscape, still changing and causing change in the everlasting now. Pinpointing the age of a rock tends to isolate it to the backwaters of the past, denying its ongoing interactions with the present.

Besides, numerical facts, no matter how incontrovertible, reveal little about the nonlinear, contingent events of Earth's history, nor about the timeless processes encapsulated by its stonework. Rocks are quiet and still, but not silent, ever, as many believe. There is abounding memory inside of stone ledge to be shared with those who care to listen. But one's mind has to go far away before the stones' murmurs can be experienced.

How can we sense deep time and represent those feelings to ourselves and to others? Encoded in our DNA molecules are vestiges of our species' evolutionary journey since life first emerged on Earth some 3.8 billion years ago. These remarkable molecular inscriptions within the human genome, consisting of about thirty-six thousand genes, connect us to everything memorable in "time's keep," as the lyricist Simon Armitage describes the deep past.

Time, stone, and self when melded into a self-similar whole allow an encounter with one's authentic being rooted to the long now that is the fountainhead of deep time. The stones are everything that we are and will ever be, all that primordial stuff flourishing deep inside of us, we 'post-modern' *Homo sapiens*.

Combining this assertion with the self-similar properties of Earth, it follows that mind without body cannot be mind; body without habitat cannot be body; habitat without ecosystem cannot be habitat; ecosystem without landscape cannot be ecosystem; and landscape without deep time cannot be landscape. And so a Cro-Magnon artist some 15 to 20 thousand years ago painted the body of a bison over a weathered protuberance of rock in an Altamira cave of the northern Spanish coast. This human, I'm convinced, had felt the 'time's keep' of the stone and used the timelessness of its everlasting now – its spirit – to animate his creation.

Given the imperious demands of modern life regulated precisely by the clock's scaffolding, why bother – waste time as some would put it – contemplating the intricacies of deep time. After all, the moments of the 21st century are what we inhabit and not the multi-billion-year expansiveness of the geologic past. Earth's history, although intriguing, is done with and has little relevance for today's globalized economic and technological systems that enervate the human-sized world.

In an essay called *Folly's Antidote*, the historian Arthur Schlesinger Jr. cautioned that "...a nation denied a conception of the past will be disabled in dealing with its present and future." This neglect of history will lead to "delusions of omnipotence and omniscience." Schlesinger is undoubtedly correct. However, his conception of history, being restricted to the last few millennia, is narrowly conceived, and represents an updated version of Arnold Toynbee's cyclical theory of human history, whereby civilizations flourished and eventually collapsed under political, economic, and ecological duress.

But that's hardly the genuine story. The anthropocentric notions expounded by Toynbee and Schlesinger are affiliations with short-term cycles that dissipated out of the everlasting now and thickened the expansiveness of the deep past. There is nothing new here. The fossil record is replete with the waning and waxing of populations, species, and biodiversity, countless events of local exterminations and global extinctions transformed into stonecrops. As Paul Shepard emphasizes in *Coming Home to the Pleistocene*, "(Western) history declares independence from origins and from "nature," which is outside the human domain except as materials and the subject of science."

I'm convinced that only through the full awareness of the deep past and the complexity of the long now can the turbulent state of 21st-century humans make any sense at all, because Nature's ways are far more dominant and pervasive than the moral guise of civilization. What lies ahead for humans are contingencies and phase transitions, and not, as many implore, a flourishing, global economy fated to grow forever. We need to live in real time, because the 21st century is very old, and is not separated from the deep geologic past except in our minds. As I see it, we are destroying ourselves by suppressing our essential wildness and natural spirit. It's a question of dignity and humility. As Cicero, a 1st century B.C. Roman statesman, proclaimed, "Not to know what happened before one was born is always to be a child."

DEEP TIME'S TRANSFORMATIONS

> "We imagine we can come to understand even the unknowable. But what we call reality begins and ends with language. Our little understanding, I now know, cannot reach beyond the limits of our two eyes and ears; our one mouth."
>
> Ana Menendez, 2009, *The Last War*

My first direct encounter with the reality of deep time occurred during a four-month-long ramble through the Dry Valleys of Antarctica. Initially, I felt abandoned and adrift in this frozen continent, as if the world had ended. On windless days, there was no sound whatsoever except for my crunchy footfalls and reflexive breathing. Lost in thought, I sensed the hardness of rock and the softness of time, features so different and yet self-similar.

Eventually, the fog in my thoughts burnt off. I intuited that the vast, barren landscapes of Antarctica represent quietness and vitality, calmness and vigor, openness and closure. Time, in the vastness of that Antarctic light felt static and seemed unable to segue forward into the newness of the future. What lurks here is not silence. Rather it is majestic stillness that is infinitely abstract, more about presence as quality rather than quantity. I finally understood that this massive, frozen continent is not so much ancient, as it is ageless, indifferent to anything and everything.

One day while scampering over a glacial moraine, I saw boulders falling off a faraway cliff, the chaotic breakdown and thunderous sounds disturbing the glassy stillness of the frozen sky. It is then that I realized that deep time incorporates rapid events (e.g., a rock slide, ice fall) alongside slow events (e.g., the opening and closing of an ocean basin), including the mid-scalar processes lodged between these two polar extremes (e.g., rainfall, tides, human life, speciation, climate change, mountain building).

Later that day safely in my tent, I remember pondering the complexity of deep time. Is the stillness of deep time mostly oscillating between rapid moments of change and absolute stasis? Do the fast, short-lived bundles of kinetic energy that flow through large landscapes texture deep time with local energy bumps? Time changes everything, but is it really change that marks time? Are we simultaneously the "instrument" for sensing deep time and the "singularity" of what deep time can become? Is deep time ever "unbalanced?" On and on it went – expressive queries without responses.

Although many people understand time as a nebulous presence impossible to characterize absolutely, most agree that it may be sensed indirectly through change. Ecologists realize that ecosystems worldwide undergo incessant transformations over time, consisting of innumerable, interacting parts and processes that are in constant flux and mutability. Among Earth's diverse, energetic ecosystems, time "streams" into the future with intensities, rhythms, surges, slow downs, swirls, and disarrays, all these temporal activities occurring at dissimilar rates simultaneously. Such energetics are radically different in the interior of Antarctica, where change is difficult to discern, its primordial landscapes seemingly frozen into place by the slowness of deep time. Here, the background of deep time is in the foreground, its diffusion settled into rock-hard stillness and mostly imperceptible change.

The opaqueness of Antarctic's deep time, I eventually came to understand, is sensed rather than intellectualized. I experienced its tempo as a crushing tranquility, a physical embodiment of a pervasive quietness – the unbounded within the bounded, the external within the internal. At such moments, everything about and within me was infused into a sublime wholeness without edges and parts, an experience comparable, I believe, to Heidegger's "happening of truth." Justin Cronin's addresses this paradoxical perspective of time in his novel *The Summer Guest*. He wrote: "The final unmaking of time, all its solid, familiar order undone, so that even the rhythm of day and night has lost its meaning and one is everywhere in one's life at once."

It seems to me that deep time is its singular self and nothing less.

Its emergent qualities are impossible to disentangle because of their interminable "slowness." Furthermore, deep time is overfilled with obscure, intertwined fabrics of chaotic existence that are the result of countless, unknowable contingencies. I recall well the times when the ageless majesty of Antarctica's mountains and ice sheet overwhelmed my persona. Those were breathless moments when I ceased to exist and so was transformed into a nonbeing.

Given these temporal complexities, how can geologists possibly probe Earth's deep time? As Zia Haider Rahman claims in his book *In the Light of What We Know*, "Reality has no way to force itself on us, and we can, in fact, alter what we think we perceive in order to suit what we want to believe." And so geologists search for physical patterns within the complex stonework of Earth. Because everything about complex reality interpenetrates time, they have to isolate and focus on the parts *that are observable and solvable* and, hence, amenable to the reductive approach of scientific inquiry. And so manifestations discerned from the detailed study of rock units are torn out of their chaotic matrices and bound together into a straight-forward chronicle of Earth's vast geological transformations, despite knowing well that the world is chaotically confusing and impossible to disassemble in any real sense. Geologists ignore this and separate out linear, cause-and-effect patterns that are used as templates for interpreting and organizing the other countless, confusing aspects of rock sequences. Yet, simplification is the antithesis of deep time.

We will never know deep time for what it actually is, because we cannot know it. According to Bryan Magee in *Ultimate Questions*, "In our attempts to understand the empirical world, we cannot get outside the empirical world. In our attempts to understand ourselves as human beings, we cannot get outside of ourselves as human beings." Consequently, the human narration of the origin of Earth's crustal rocks cannot reveal deep time as it really exists. What does this avowal mean exactly?

Some decades ago, I had read Marc Auge's *Oblivion*, a treatise that examines the origin of memory. He claims that human memory is not what we choose to remember about the past. Rather our memories, he argues, are created by everything that we erase. The flotsam that is left remains in our mind and becomes the memory of all the events that each of us recalls. In addition, the deep obscurities of deep time involve the concept of loss due to erosion of strata and their entombed fossils, as well as loss of the full record of the species diversity of the past due to the acute rarity of fossilization. As such, we have reconstructed an evolutionary history of life on Earth, despite the absence of fossil evidence for the vast majority of species that were once alive.

Such truthful insights led me to reevaluate critically Darwin's theory of evolution by natural selection. We know well that evolutionary novelty unfolds across a wide range of spatial and temporal scales, a renewal of life from death far too pervasive, far too chancy, and far too shadowy to predict. Furthermore, some paleontologists now suspect that the notion of loss (oblivion and erosion) is preeminent in the evolutionary dynamics of speciation. Hence, the forces that drive the transformation of species are not so much about selection of the fittest as about 'deselection' of the least fit. When environments change, the least fit individuals die off, removing forever their DNA from their species' gene pool.

There is additional hard evidence supporting the importance of loss in creating newness. For example, Henry Gee's in his recent book *The Accidental Species: Misunderstandings of Human Evolution* affirms emphatically: "Most of what seems to be going on in evolution is not the acquisition of new, improved ways of living, but their wholesale loss." So, if correct, this implies that Nature does not select; rather it 'deselects' in the same way that human memory is realized. Moreover, Philip Reno, a biomedical scientist, asserted in a recent paper *Missing Links* that "Our big human brains, upright gait and style of love may exist because we shed pieces of DNA." In other words gene deletion may have been the cause of human divergence from the great apes and not the large size of our brain.

Paradoxically, the forces that unmake systems are those that create them. There is no 'survival of the *fittest*' in such a world, but only the 'survival of the *fitter*,' and merely for the blink of an eye. Implausibly, the species comprising the communities of today's landscapes, including *Homo sapiens*, co-evolved by chance out of an uncertain backdrop of eco-evolutionary bedlam even though the foreground seen with half-shut eyes makes it appear as if it was fated to happen.

What lies ahead? The long haul of the ages will certainly outlast humans, regardless of how earnestly we clench our hands or fill our minds with fantastical dreams of our species singularity as a transcendent being.

The ordinary world is much deeper than people's yearning and heart. The life of the ancient past is gone, mostly extinct, a tiny fraction of it having flash-lit into a today of bacteria, fungi, birches, elks, wolves, and humans.

This is *Homo sapiens*' joyous moment in the sun. Ahead is a deep, capricious future of chaos and contingencies, overfilled with close- and far-flung disturbances, no lasting equilibria, and countless lost causes. Besides, the sun so inhumanly stoic will someday bloat into a red giant and then, long after the oceans are boiled away and Earth is bleached of life, will wither into a white dwarf.

In a world fated to end in the faraway emergence of the Deep Future, there really are no antagonists except for our panic-stricken minds. After all, as a character exclaims in Cormac McCarthy's novel *The Road*: "People were always getting ready for tomorrow. I didn't believe in that. Tomorrow wasn't getting ready for them. It didn't even know they were there."

Clearly, everything that we are has materialized out of the effluvium of the eternal now. At birth, we emerge from deep complexity and at death we disintegrate into deep complexity. We are simultaneously a cognizant being able to sense deep time and a singular elaboration of its complexity. No story, including our own, has a beginning or an end, because time is bundled energy overfilled with contingency from which the moment's existence perpetually unfolds. Moreover, the history of each entity of the world, small and large – its transformative existence in the eternal now – is both singular and self-similar at the same time. And it is this interconnected space/time complexity internalized by humans, which connects us to the entire world and validates are use of metaphorical language and symbolic art to describe our surroundings to ourselves.

Lakoff and Johnson emphasize in *Philosophy in the Flesh* that most of human cognition, about 95% of it, is unconscious and not accessible to reason. Our thoughts, both conscious and unconscious, emerge out of the complicated neural biochemistry of our embodied brain. Terry Eagleton in a book review entitled *I Am, Therefore I Think* stated boldly: "Our rationality and animality are bound tightly together." He continues: "Am I my body, or am I more than it?....The problem is that we both are, and are not, our bodies. We are more than them – but not in the sense of being something different from them."

Geologists have a long perspective of Earth's complex past, all of which had to occur in order for me to write this essay and for you to read it. Stewart Brand in his book *The Clock of the Long Now: Time and Responsibility* asserts: "The slow stuff is the serious stuff, but it is invisible to us quick learners. Our senses and our thinking habits are turned to what is sudden, and oblivious to anything gradual....What happens fast is illusion, what happens slow is reality." So, how should we be thinking about the deep future?

There are no answers; only questions. There is no understanding; only ignorance. There are no solutions of consequence; only immense spans of unformed time. However, we do know for sure that the future includes each of our deaths. As the deep future is absorbed into the deep past, it will be as unique and complex as our current past. As such, it is imperative that we adapt self-effacingly to whatever emerges as Earth self-organizes itself a day at a time.

PART III
Reverberations of Deep Time

MOUNTAINS AND THE MIND

"We are now in the mountains and they are in us, kindling enthusiasm, making every nerve quiver, filling every pore and cell of us."

John Muir, 1911, *My First Summer in the Sierra*

Mountains mesmerize. The starkness of spine-backed ridges, the incongruity of their cracked glaciers and shattered ledge, and the habits of frozen days can provoke biting despair. Individuals who scamper up and down steep ice and cliff faces are reminded of the precariousness of life and the finality of death. Mountains begrudge us nothing. Rather, they join us face-to-face with impermanence, with existence forever unraveling into nothingness.

I took notice of this counsel and began to spend part of my life embracing the tempestuous wildness of mountains. There, in the rudimentary world of snow, ice, and stone, I learned to listen rather than to speak and to feel rather than to think. From time to time while seeking purchase on a steep ridgeline, I encountered the amorality of the eons, instants when the combined weight of insignificance and non-meaning penetrated my mind such that my life became whole. Eventually, I reclaimed for myself what Erazin Kohak called "the gifts of darkness, solitude, and pain."

I've spent more long nights in a small tent being mauled by heavy wind than I can bring to mind. I was deeply afraid every time. The freight-train roar of wind in free fall, the pelting of sleet and snow, the machine-gun snap of tent fabric create a wildness of sound that is indescribable in its rawness. The air howls and shrieks as if mad, and lays down hard-packed snowdrifts. The tent – overfilled with darkness, climbing gear, and sleepless bodies – expands and compresses like a bellows. Heartbeats, heavy breathing, and annoying coughs lay down bits of time. Incredibly, the razor-thin fabric of my tent is all that separates my life from my death.

Not quite asleep, not quite awake, I'm glad that I'm not alone. I'm told that you can be driven insane in such circumstances. So I gaze into the worried eyes of my climbing companions and wonder about my own fears. When the wind moans its fury, I've learned that there's nothing to be done, and so my mind settles to a bottommost state. My thoughts become whispers, my life bare. I cultivate patience and get heavy doses of humility. For these graces, I am truly indebted to the fierceness of towering peaks.

Once free of a storm-battered tent, my mind, starved for sensation, awakens and longs for splendor. Mountains with their girth and height, and boundless light, rarely disappoint. In such stony stillness, my eyes are wider than my mind. I inhale and exhale the edgeless patterns of ice cliffs gleaming in the sunshine, as cloud shadow dapples the crusty surface of snow pack. Far below, I see long inclines of glaciers burning in the sun and bleeding from cupric blue crevasses. High above, the graceful parabolic curve of a cirque wall joins the backbone of ridgelines, softening the ragged contours of their weathered ledge.

Somehow the primal blend deep inside knots of stone and ice are keenly metaphysical. Joy overwhelms me at such moments. D. H. Lawrence knew this. In *Apocalypse* he wrote: "For man, as for flower and beast and bird, the supreme triumph is to be most vividly, most perfectly alive…We ought to dance with rapture that we should be alive and in the flesh, and part of the living incarnate cosmos. I am part of the sun as my eye is part of me. That I am part of the Earth, my feet know perfectly, and my blood is part of the sea." Such unpretentious appearances of reality cannot be imagined; they can only be sensed and internalized.

Yet, mountains are extremely dangerous in countless, unforeseen ways. I remember a long-ago snowstorm with horrific winds pummeling the tall peaks of the Himalayas. The monsoon season apparently had lingered longer than usual. Finally, it ended and now blessed sunshine caressed our bodies and minds. I was mesmerized by the stillness of lofty peaks everywhere above me. My thoughts were slowly slipping backwards into the deepness of the geologic past.

Abruptly, a sonic blast shattered the quietness of the late morning.

The far side of Ama Dablan was avalanching. The deafening sonic boom was extreme, as huge slabs of rock, ice, and snow were avalanching down a narrow ravine cut into the mountainside. Although we were safely encamped on an abutting arête, a huge, dense cloud of fine snow raised by the avalanche was rapidly approaching us. We rushed into our tents and quickly zipped them closed. The snow cloud enveloped us; nothing but the skin of our tents prevented our lungs from filling with snow. Climbers drown in such conditions.

Despite such perils, I discovered that traipsing in mountains away from the world of material contentment has made me clear-headed and aware of the animal nature of my true humanity. Now, I've become, as Kohak describes, "...*homo humanus*...who no longer simply asks, "Do I like it?" but "Is it beautiful?," not simply "Is it useful?" but rather "Is it good?," not merely "How do I feel about it?" but rather "Is it right?"" Moreover, I came to realize that reaching the summit of huge, ageless mountains is not what should matter to mountaineers. Rather, the process of climbing with colleagues, sharing fear and joy, anguish and contentment, amidst the raw, uncaring wildness of mountains is how one can learn to embrace one's mortality.

One tragedy of modern existence is that we no longer can or, worse yet, even care to discern the depth and grace of our existential animal being, each of us, alone and together, inhabitants of a spinning Earth, orbiting in the Solar System and swirling in the Milky Way. Ensconced in the rational world of cityscapes, we mistakenly intellectualize our evolutionary past as *Homo sapiens* and proclaim that we are now transcendent beings.

Jack Turner in *The Abstract Wild* reminds us that "(w)e only value what we know and love, and we no longer know or love the wild. So instead we accept substitutes, imitations, semblances, and fakes – a diminished wild." Many people strive to outsmart the shared ecology of mountains and blindly pursue the conquest of peaks. Such supreme thoughts about the self have led to disastrous fallout, including the desecration of remote mountains everywhere on Earth.

Emblematic of these attitudes, mountaineering crises are emerging each year at the base of Mount Everest, a huge, three-walled pyramid that soars ~8,848 meters (29,028 feet) above sea level. Named Sagarmatha by the Nepalese and Chomolungma by the Tibetans, Sherpas regard the entire surrounding massif as sacred land, and so the bases of the high Himalayan peaks are graced with prayer flags and Buddhist monasteries.

In the mid-20th century, expeditions to reach the summit of Sagarmatha were few in number. Today, hundreds of people are drawn to base camp, where parties are legendary, where gear, equipment, and food are stolen, and where electronic devices and even espresso machines abound. Sherpas do most of the hauling of the equipment to this western-dominated playground.

Nowadays, there are several climbing companies who hire guides to lead clients to the summit for a sizable cost. Most of the customers are in good physical shape, but many have little experience at ascending high-altitude peaks. These are mostly people unable or unwilling to become legitimate mountaineers on their own. What they want is "to bag this peak now!"

Among boastful socialites, ascending Sagarmatha somehow has become a highly regarded achievement. The result of these activities is excessive consumption of limited resources, the buildup of garbage heaps littering base camp, and inappropriate behavior that offends Sherpas as well as the mountain. Tragically, more than 280 climbers have died on Sagarmatha, their frozen bodies scattered about the climbing routes.

I recall well the moment when I ascended an icefall on the Khumbu glacier and was brusquely chastised by a full view of Sagarmatha's girth and height. Incredibly, the mountain is still growing upward and moving northward several centimeters per year, as a consequence of lithospheric plate collisions between India and Asia. Two of its rock faces were visible, each sharply gouged by erosion, their ledge packed with snow, their gullies filled with alpine glaciers. A long spindrift streaming off its peak reached into the Jet Stream. Average summer temperatures at the summit are below zero degrees Fahrenheit. It was impossible not to feel insignificant as the mountain's immense shadow coldly embraced me.

Sargarmatha, despite its hugeness, will not exist forever. Neither will *Homo sapiens*. As Jeffrey Kiehl avows in *Facing Climate Change*, "(The) perspective on who we are and how we exist in the world rests on the observation that we are not separate beings. There is no way to cut the invisible cords tying us to our surroundings, and this becomes more apparent when our surroundings change….(to) push the world around at will is an illusion."

Some believe that we are now living in the "Century of the Environment," an age when we will be obligated to confront our history of pillaging ecosystems everywhere – degrading habitats and exterminating biota – to serve our own material ends, while disavowing any ethical responsibility as a profligate species of Earth's biosphere. Our long-standing habits of violence and destruction have compromised mountainscapes, and these changes are extreme for the planet.

As a geologist, I do believe strongly in radical hope, because Earth systems will outlive our species presence and will be rejuvenated with populations of diverse new life forms that we cannot imagine. This, for me, is a reassuring outcome, a deep future once again filled with ecological rapture that supersedes the diminished era of human existence.

WHAT AM I?

"I am so hungry for something real."

Rick Bass, 2006, *The Lives of Rocks: Stories*

Consider what it means to live in one's body. The question, a philosophically complicated one, has engaged thinkers for millennia and continues to do so. Allow me to 'unthink' the question by resorting to the effectual power of empirical science to reveal how a human is physically put together.

An adult's body consists of about ten trillion cells, a quantity that is obscure unless one ponders its hugeness. If you were to count from one to ten trillion, enunciating one number per second, it would take over 30,000 years to complete this not-so-simple task, a time interval that would span across some 650 generations! By anyone's accounting, this allotment of cells in the human body is colossal, far beyond what's familiar and comprehensible. From so little, the fusion of egg and sperm, comes so much – a breathing, sweating, yearning biped endowed with a self-conscious mind stunned by how she came to be.

Now, apprise the aggregate number of atoms that constitute the ten trillion cells of the human body. It's beyond reason really, and yet large numbers of these body atoms are replaced every day, all of them within ten years, such that we don a spanking new birthday suit each and every decade of our lives. And every bit of this fresh atomic material is derived ultimately from outside the body, mined unconsciously by breathing, drinking, and eating chemicals released by the weathering of rocks. And yet despite the rejuvenating genius of this ecologic act, memory – our language, imagination, thoughts, opinions, and delusions – is somehow chemically retained in the neural networks crimped into the brain's gray matter. Surely, we speak out of the biochemical virtuosity of our cells, making the wild molecules of air gathered in our voice boxes sing out melodies of expressive glee or grief whenever we are so inclined.

Christopher Uhl in *Developing Ecological Consciousness* and Robert Buckman in *Human Wildlife* describe the cellular and microbial makeup of people. Altogether the human physique harbors some one hundred trillion cells, a mere tenth of which are the body units discussed above. The remaining ninety percent, 90 trillion cells, are aliens at first glance, teeming populations of diverse microorganisms that inhabit the body's hideaways. They flourish in unimaginable numbers on the skin, eyes, and ears, and on the hair and in the follicles of the scalp, eyebrows, nose, and armpits. They've invaded the mouth, covering its lips, gums, teeth, and tongue with robust communities of bacteria, essentially biofilms that Buckman maintains are the "equivalent of a growing city."

These multitudes of microbes have claimed ownership of our respiratory, gastrointestinal and urinary tracts, and are lodged in every nook and cranny of our interior landscape. They swirl about, their presence texturing our breath and fluids, enfolded deeply into our being, perhaps even into the recesses of our soul. In a word, their world, the reality of their existence, is our body, and some two hundred species of microbes – bacteria, viruses, fungi – as well as numerous multicellular organisms – ticks, chiggers, lice, fleas, nematodes, tapeworms, and other wildlife – have contented lives, as they idle, feed, defecate, and reproduce in the biosphere of our bodies. What does it mean exactly to live in a body that is not strictly our own, that is shared with ninety trillion other creatures?

Holding on to the significance of population numbers without end is no easy matter. Chris Uhl points out that the throngs of the bacterium *Escherichia coli* (familiarly known as *E. coli*) encamped in the twisted interior of your gut, if laid out front to end, would traverse the continental United States, an invisible microbial chain stretched out across the vastness of the Appalachians, the Great Plains, and the Continental Divide. Imagine yourself driving from Boston to Seattle, humming the whole way to hold tightly to the vision of this invisible transcontinental lineup of your *E. coli*, remembering that these numberless hordes of living microbes are along for the trip packed safely away in the paunch of your belly.

Even more farfetched is the aggregate number of microorganisms that dwell in the bodies of the entire human race. Although the calculation is a direct one [(9 x 10^{13} microbes/person) (7 x 10^9 people) = 63 x 10^{22} microbes], the result – the number sixty-three followed by twenty-two zeroes – is dizzying, a godlike quantity that should be orbiting rather than resting upon the Earth. Somehow, the world becomes heavier to bear and understand with the knowledge of the hidden micro-details of our personal biology.

Even the unconscious act of breathing, the joining and untangling of air molecules in the respiratory tract of our bodies, is as miraculous as the awakening light at the cusp of a reborn day. Chris Uhl writes: "Breathing is a mind-boggling activity……The air you have breathed in is chock-full of molecules, bringing you detailed information about your surroundings – sometimes stimulating your appetite, arousing you, warning you, and perhaps even triggering deep emotions and distant memories. The air goes into your throat, where it enters the trachea, which soon branches and sends "pipes" to each of your lungs. Within your lungs, the notion of boundaries, inside and outside, blurs as the planet's atmosphere enters your bloodstream on a massive scale."

Uhl then makes known the fullness of the chemical fluxes associated with the splendor of breathing air. Remarkably, during *every single minute of our lives*, twenty-five billion red blood cells, each accommodating 350 million hemoglobin molecules, course through the intricate byways of our lungs. There, across a delicate membrane, carbon dioxide gets exchanged for oxygen to the end of our days as assuredly as the repetition of the moon-drawn tides. And not just air stirs deep within us but ocean water as well. Almost seventy percent of our solid body, those trillions of cells that are you and I, is the impounded flowage of tidewater. Our insides are actually afloat in an expanse of ocean, our bodies' virtual water gardens of delight. The poet Jaan Kaplinski characterizes this state as "the same sea in us all."

This back-and-forth surge of chemical compounds is the opulence of life, whether it is the slime of pond scum or a pride of lions, whether it is the slight nuance of an invisible bacterium or the muscularity of the human brain in thought. These universal parallels are responsible for the symphonies of life everywhere on Earth.

And so why are we so discomfited with our animal connections such that many regard our shared evolutionary past as a trifling scientific fact that no longer matters now and for the foreseeable time to come? Why do we insist that people alone have the freedom of reverential brilliance, which makes us the "who" and everything else alive the "what?" Why do we declare that the visionary strength of our intellect, imagination, and technologies has rubbed out the capricious and whimsical habits of the wild from our cultured lives except in our bad dreams? Why is the Western mindset so maniacally obsessed with control, to give only cities and market economies their way, and to reason that we alone control our fate? How does one respond to such self-serving proclamations of words that disavow the glaringly obvious, that the primeval forces which created us are also devouring our bodies and minds, turning their chemical bits back into the vast compost of the indifferent soil that will be our ending place?

Those who ponder such matters believe that recognizing our human animalism, admitting that like mushrooms, snails, and snakes we are no more than the purposeless aftereffect of biological evolution, subverts the truth of our moral law and undermines our rightful place in God's embrace. Daniel Dennett writes in *Darwin's Dangerous Idea* that people are aghast at the biological explication of *Homo sapiens* on the grounds that it "explain(s) away the Minds and Purposes and Meanings that we all hold dear." Steven Pinker agrees. In *The Blank Slate: The Modern Denial of Human Nature*, he makes plain the conviction of most people that "....if our joys and satisfactions are just biochemical events that will someday sputter out for good, if life was not created for a higher purpose and directed toward a noble goal, then why go on living?" This helps explain, I suppose, why today more than forty percent of adult Americans choose to forget or reject outright our "beastly" evolutionary origin. Such a half-asleep reaction of well-muscled minds to logic is distressing and reproaches the outer truth of our inner life.

We seem to fear our evolutionary emergence, because mere subservience to the physical and biological cycles of Earth seems to sully our august existence. For millennia in the West, human dignity and self-worth have been defined by words in opposition to the imputed lock-step trappings of evolution and ecology. After all, people insist, we are infinitely more than muscle and bone, and mere instinctual subject. At death's door we do transcend the material ordinariness of Earth's landscape and rise above the permanently grounded nature of the planet. All of that may be true, but yet, as Erazim Kohak insists in *The Embers and the Stars,* "Humans cannot live at peace with themselves and their God if they are not at peace with nature."

Truth, we all agree, demands respect and needs to be faced squarely, if we are to claim legitimacy as a rational, moral being, if our loose daydreams and the silent offerings of our deaths are to be anchored to reality. "Know thyself" for what you are instead of what you pretend yourself to be. After all, trivial habits of the mind have never led to the deep awareness of biological existence. Beginning with what can be observed and confirmed by experience not only compensates for the free-form habits of our imagination, but also provides a relational context that can be trusted for framing what human nature actually is. Having said this, however, I suspect that even the best words aren't enough to accord with the confounding depth and timbre of our interior being and our collective existence.

The findings of evolutionary biology and ecology are quite explicit in this respect. For example, it is fact that science has uncovered no supremely unique atomic ingredient in our physical makeup, a logic that acknowledges the kindred continuity between Earth and all life forms including us. Also it is clear that a complex shared ecology is stamped on the whole biology of our being, in both the body and the mind. Lynn Margulis and Dorian Sagan argue in *What Is Life?* that "Thought, like life, is matter and energy in flux; the body is its 'other side.' Thinking and being are the same thing." In other words, we have been naturally selected and, hence, are graceful accidents of evolutionary circumstance. Beast and human and nature are one and the same.

The discoveries of modern science are clear: humans are not freestanding, blue-blooded beings, but are a species of animal that is deeply embedded in the natural ecology of the world. We, *Homo sapiens*, are part of the biological universe despite the demurral of our ego, culture, and language, which are choking on the dream that humans are divine and, hence, privileged ends in themselves. As Friedrich Nietzsche posed, "Has not all philosophy been a misunderstanding of the body?"

Am I my body? It seems that I am, because I did not exist until my body was sexually conceived and born into the world. Is my body exclusively my own? After all, I wash it, groom it, dress it, give it medicine and rest when it is sick, and marry another body to create children's bodies that I name and claim as my own. When young I watch my body ripen with anticipation and pride, when old with longing and concern; eventually I arrange to have my body buried or cremated after it is, and therefore I am, dead.

So, firsthand knowledge indicates that my body and I are each other. But as astonishing as my carnal being seems to be, the present question is: Is self-experienced existence really as uncomplicated as the birth, aging, and death of my body, as simple as what Erazim Kohak calls a philosophy of personalism? Am I more than me? Is there in fact a ghostly side to the fallow contours of my being? Science proclaims guilelessly that there most assuredly is.

To begin, the cells everywhere in and on our body get replaced habitually without conscious regulation. Everything about us is forever changing; becoming is incessant. We breathe in countless molecules of air and exhale comparable quantities of breath every instant of our lives. We drink water and eat food, and reciprocate by sweating, urinating, and defecating a complex chemical stew of gases, liquids and solids into the enveloping ecosystems. Molecular morsels of our lungs, liver, heart, and brain, bits from every part of our physical self, its insides and outsides, become the stuff of sumptuous feasts for trees, worms, and voles, for porcupines, moose, and wolves.

Being and becoming are everlasting. What's more, our skin, which we conceive as a boundary surface separating the deep interior space of the self from everything else around, a private self-enclosure so to speak, is trespassed with impunity by the give-and-take of chemical exchange with the surrounding environment every moment that we are alive. If these plenteous biochemical transactions did not occur, we would be utterly lifeless stuff. So in some sense, the claim that my body and its life are sharply edged and exclusively my own is mistaken. Rather there is no self-reliant privacy for anything that lives, because organisms are always open to the life-giving benevolence of the natural world. Margulis and Sagan make plain this very point: "The question "What is life?" is thus a linguistic trap. To answer according to the rules of grammar, we must supply a noun, a thing. But life on Earth is more like a verb. It repairs, maintains, recreates, and outdoes itself."

The cells of life are not singular *objects in space* but rather integrated *processes through time*, edgeless and ceaseless breaths of energy, water, gases, and solids that pulsate biochemically in ways that are far more playful than Newton's staid laws of planetary motions. In the finitude of the biological Earth, the action of death, including yours and mine, is not an end, but a preparatory shadow for ecological rebirth. We die and then in still life we putrefy into compost. Thereafter our sweetness brightens the greenness of new leaves and the wetness of young saplings. In death as well as life, and like everything alive, we are all masterpieces of ecological art.

Nothing alive is genuinely individualistic and self-reliant. Even our distinctive physical traits evident in the backward glance of a mirror deceive. What we are at heart is not simple and plain. According to Lynn Margulis, if every one of our ten trillion body cells were suddenly to vanish, our three-dimensional form would still stand out in ghostly silhouette because of the still-remaining ninety trillion microbes that inhabit each of our bodies. When we embrace our child or lover, we are mostly touching those other things. So, what am I really, if I am one and they are ninety trillion? But life is not dichotomous. It is not they and I. It is we together, our mutual virtuosity, that flames up the life in the body that I am. No one can ever be other than this collective biological self that each of us is.

So, if what underscores my life is not bone-quiet as it appears to be, the question "What am I exactly?" is left begging. The first reasonable step for explaining myself is to put aside the chimera of self-love, and become authentically open to the narratives of modern ecology.

It is given that my embodied being is the home place of trillions of tiny living things, homesteaders that by their lodgment claim to be the otherness of me. From their perspective, my body is an anatomical terrain with topographic twists and turns that run up and down the curved hills and furrows of my insides. Air and water course through the landscape crevices of my interior-self, creating daily weather and seasonal climate that become pulsating breaths of expressive feeling, perception, and imagining. These microbes cannot live without me or I without them. We are intertwined into a transcendent whole that is more mysterious and grander than each of us alone could ever be. This co-existence derived from the stone strength and bog scum of the evolutionary past bestows meaning and magnificence to *Homo sapiens* as well as to the marrow of the deep nonhuman future that is yet to be realized by ceaseless and ungraspable evolutionary elaborations.

It seems to me that the crucial meaning of the crowded, high country filling our insides is self-evident and must not remain unnoticed. Each of us is a flourishing ecosystem, not metaphorically, but literally. Bits of rock, drops of water, drafts of air enter and leave our bodies incessantly, providing nutriment to the ghostly biota communing upon and below the ground of our flesh. Our cells are nested in a tissue, our tissues in an organ, our organs in a body much like Russian dolls snuggled comfortably into one another. However, unlike these dolls, which are empty shells, we are not, for we are overfilled with the ever-blooming lushness of hidden microbial communities. Margulis and Sagan say it well: "The strength of symbiosis as an evolutionary force undermines the prevalent notion of individuality as something fixed, something secure and sacred. A human being in particular is not single, but a composite. Each of us provides a fine environment for bacteria, fungi, roundworms, mites, and others that live in and on us....Our bodies are actually joint property of the descendants of diverse ancestors."

Each of us is an earth within Earth. Our body has the contours of mountains and the motion of rivers and sea tides, and we share it with some 200 species of microbes. As Diane Ackerman writes, "Think of a niche and life will fill it, think of a shape and life will explore it, think of a drama and life will stage it." We are all ecological stories, each of us a miniaturized habitat well outside the range of common sense. But not for the ninety trillion microbes spread across and inside our bodies that live lives of eating, reproducing, and dying, which in turn allows you and me to eat, reproduce, and die.

So these very words and thoughts that I've transcribed to these pages, the wonderful things that excite my mind, are the microbes' doings as well as my own. I feel sure that this is where the sciences join the arts, because beauty, imagination, reason, and love are rooted in the fertile soil of untold ecological unions where microbes, flesh, and spirit get combined.

This means, of course, that I am wild even while walking among the stampeding crowds of downtown Manhattan, an engineered metropolis of exquisitely sculpted concrete and metal seemingly, but really not, far away from the loose windage of forested mountains. The wild is not just elsewhere, a place outside of us that we can think about and visit on occasion. Rather it is the whole of what we are and can ever be. And so I smile deep inside, because all is right with the single stream of ecological beauty that courses naturally within each of our beings.

OF DYING AND BECOMING

"But there's no point separating yourself from the earth with a stone wall after you are dead. A person lives from the earth, and they should give their eternity back to the earth. The earth deserves something from people too."

Wieslaw Mysliwski, 1999, *Stone Upon Stone*, (English translation 2010 by Bill Johnson)

I often visit a small forest glade near my home in upstate New York where eccentric stones grow out of the ground. The sandstone blocks, rough cut and moss daubed, lie knocked about every which way as if having been struck by a whimsical storm. Heavy-trunked hardwoods, their bark deeply creased and split by weather, lean their twisted branches towards the fallen stones and jack up the sky. Their damp shadows sit heavy and still. On the ground, waist-thick elbows torn off of ancient maples serve as raised beds of compost for new plants to grow. As night fades into morning, ribbons of sunshine drip off the forest canopy, the disheveled stones shining and darkening in the shiver of dawn-light. This place, almost forgotten, is an old, walled-in boneyard where nineteenth-century bodies were laid down to rot and flame up the soil.

Nothing much seems to happen from year to year in this burial ground. The graveyard's access is unremarkable, merely a foot trail of gummy mud that branches off a dusty logging road. Two wooden placards nailed to evergreens mark its entryway. Each panel is inscribed simply with a yellow cross, one older and faded, the other newer and lavish. From the entranceway, the path skirts a confusion of undergrowth and drops down to the tight meander curl of a creek that is eating hungrily into the graveyard's memories. The brook gathers water from the sky and from seeps that flow down a broad bedrock swell to the west, and sweeps silt, sand, and leaf detritus to a narrow, swampy floodplain. I'm told that people are drawn to river junctures, and this pocketsize burial ground, 22 by 32 paces of unmapped contour, reaffirms this long-held belief.

The moments come with the onrush of the brook, as swirling water murmurs secrets about long-ago lives that closed and family hearts that burst. As I think backwards to the start, to a time well before cool tombstone had replaced warm, human flesh, a glacier scraped raw the ridge-top ledges of Brookfield and plastered sticky till against its scooped-out hollows. A great ice melt followed and the glacier retreated, leaving the cold ground in shambles. Soon after, animals returned to the spruce thickets and the boggy barrens that had emerged out of the cold, embryonic soil.

Eventually, a riverine vernacular undid the placid design of this sparse woodland and created a landscape of motion. The creek's fluid tongue spewed out channel riffles, mud banks, sand bars, logjams, and riverweed bogs. These interstratified features of the creek bed got combined with sun, wind, and rain, an ecological recipe for transforming upstate New York into a deciduous forest. A mere stone's throw from the eastern edge of the gravesite, the creek transfers its sediment load to a larger stream that runs hard and surly for the sea.

The sanctity of this seamless place, where fullness embraces emptiness and wholeness, where nothing is errant or wanting, frees my mind from its abiding habits and fears. Under the wind-broken trees, I stand still and study the roughness of the graveyard and its bedload of bodies. The wayward moments spent in the coolness of the creek bog and in the ripeness of the boneyard move my thoughts in unfamiliar ways. I mull over the soaked ground of the floodplain and the graceful sweep of the creek's cutbanks. I become quiet with the splashes of light that puddle up on the gray tombstones, sowed in the ground for eternity.

With the late afternoon dip of the sun, there's a Paleolithic feel to the dim light that lays still and mute like the tombstones and the slowness of my thinking. My eyes search the long shadows of the boneyard for whispers from the past. Immersed in the sacred hours of the day, my thoughts leap forward and backward with bewilderment.

Deep presence, a sequencing of order and chaos, lingers here with names and dates stripped of accents. Headstone inscriptions partly erased by centuries of weather and smeared with crusty lichen and damp moss speak earnestly about the dead, about a time and a place before my life arrived.

Imagine the angled geometry of the stones planted in the lumpy ground beneath wind-wrangled limbs of maples under a century's worth of heavy-winter moonlight. Where exactly does the leaf mold of the graveyard end and I begin? Where are the creases between my body and the moss-grimed snags, between my imaginings and the hoarfrost glazing the boughs of hemlocks? When does my journey of leaving begin?

A tabular headstone, rising straight out of the packed myrtle, inescapably draws my mind's eye whenever I visit my long-gone neighbors. This slab of carved gritstone is almost twice as large from side to side as the other marker stones of the cemetery. Besides, the weather-stained gravestone has not one but two graceful arches sculpted into its crown, one for a woman, the other for her husband, a conjugal bas relief of Esther and Samuel Hill. A diagonal fracture slices the base so that its left edge, Esther's side, is no longer straight but doglegged. The terse words chiseled side-by-side into the grainy rock read:

OUR MOTHER *OUR FATHER*
ESTHER HILL *SAMUEL HILL*
DIED *DIED*
JULY 15, 1857 *NOV. 20, 1826*
81 YEARS, 3 MOS. &10 DAYS *55 YEARS, 10 MOS. & 5 DAYS*

Apparently, every feral moment was precious for these nineteenth-century souls, because not only the years, but also the months and days before they spent their final breath were pushed into the future as scratches on tabular stones. I imagine that existence for this graveyard couple was thin, filled with the grime of unbroken days when great maples and beeches were felled by hand, and stones jammed ox-drawn plows, when food was sparse and mealy, when clean winter air crusted the ground and eyelids alike. Remaking leafy wilderness, breaking apart glacial drift into stone-walled pastures and corn fields, tired the body until it slept; once rested or not, the body rose and toiled anew, while submerged in despairing weather, a bit too wet, much too cold, amounting to long seasons of laughter and tears, of blushing and sighing, of moping and dreaming.

I suspect that although each day dragged wearily along, the combined days of their single-minded lives rushed by like surging water spilling over a cliff edge. How comforting finally to let go of life's throes for the eternal writ of soil decay, in the end to lie down by the silver light of a gurgling creek in the forest haze of an Earth-bound heaven under a stone with writing so that no one gets forgotten. Over a lifetime the simple elegance of Esther's and Samuel's fieldstone walls and gravestone beds contoured the ledges of Brookfield with the quiet beauty of deep-felt presence.

In life, the Hills were as fertile as the land they cultivated. Esther bore three, possibly four children, maybe more. It's hard to tell exactly, because most of the eighteen headstones in the graveyard are blank, having been cleansed of letters and numbers by weather and time, a natural concession to the finitude of biological existence in life as well as in memory. The Hill's efforts at homesteading the forest and birthing a family, and their endings, which started in this boneyard, spread themselves out across countless forgotten days.

Esther buried her husband and three of her children. Polly, the first-born (1800-1854), died last at age 54, whereas Roswell, the last-born (1814-1842), died first at age 28; the two bracketed the birth and death of their sister Lydia (1806-1845), whose life ended at 39 years of age. Other than the family name, few particulars are preserved for Charles, a possible second son and fourth child of the Hill family. His modest headstone, rubbed smooth and cracked by caustic weather, is much smaller than those of his siblings, suggesting that he was hastily dug into the family plot by distant relatives or by family friends, sometime after the passing of Esther, his mother. The surviving words on his gravestone read: CHARLES, SON OF HILL, DIED....

The Hills, I imagine, had few diversions from their drawn-out workdays. Thoughts and hopes, no matter their splendor and need, swayed and bent, and in time disentangled into nothing at all by the drift of crosswinds. A small, insular community spread out over the irregularities of the land populated this narrow space of silent stars and unmarked roads, a place where you were born and died, and in the end were planted into the forest floor.

These Brookfield farms – tight clusters of broken cabins and small outbuildings – must have been a burdensome world for youngsters to endure, particularly when the fecund smells of springtime filled their bodies with sexual yearning. Nineteenth-century Brookfield, where all the doors to elsewhere were shut, was not a place for youth. Three of the Hill children – Roswell, Lydia, and Charles – never found wedlock companions. Polly, the first born, did; she married Bela Hammond who died August 31, 1860 at the age of 69 years and nine days, a mere six years after he buried his wife.

I'm not sure where exactly the Hammond graves are located underfoot, because their headstones have been lifted from somewhere and leaned back to back against the opposite sides of an ancient, black cherry tree standing sentry over the boneyard. The white gravestone of their daughter Jane lies flat on the ground near the base of this stout tree, the nearby soil covered by creeping myrtle and broken branches that were bleached by the sun and look like human bones. The death marks read:

> *AUG. 1, 1850*
> *BABY JANE*
> *DAUGHTER OF*
> *BELA & POLLY HAMMOND*
> *AGED*
> *18 YEARS, 6 MOS. & 22 DAYS*

Why, I wonder, was this 18-year-old woman buried as Baby Jane? Perhaps she suffered a congenital ailment or a childhood disease, which not only stunted her growth, but also hastily closed off her life. To Bela and Polly, their daughter remained everlastingly their Baby Jane.

The two oldest headstones in the burying plot stand side-by-side, straight as iron rods, just inside the low wall of crumbling stones by the north entrance. They belong to the Shepards, folks born more than a half-century before the country gained its 1776 independence from British sovereignty. Most likely, the Shepards were among the first homesteaders of the Brookfield wilderness.

I try to imagine what was here back then. I picture a high, green escarpment broken by ledges of gray stone and twisty trails of mud, and a summer sky muffled by the shadowed growth of maples, beeches, and hemlock. Eden for sure, the Shepards must have thought when the dawning summer sun crested the nearby ridgeline and blazed a sweep of new light across the drop of the valley floor. At least for now, ignore the cold thoughts of winter, they must have agreed. And for the first time ever in its geologic history, a tract of this rugged landscape was appropriated, cleared of growing trees and glacial boulders, and cultivated as pasture and cropland, while animals like wolves, bears, and cougars disappeared or were extirpated.

Carved into the pair of nicked and stained headstones are the words:

Mr.	Mrs.
Jonas Shepard	*Esther wife*
Died 9 of June	*of*
1807 in the 83^d	*Jonas Shepard*
yr. of his	*died Apr. 13*
age	*1816 in the*
	79 yr. of her
	age

He left this world, his toils are over
Free from all.......grief &.........

And so it appears that the deep stirrings of this boneyard, where the texture of lived time feels as weighty as granite ledge, burst forth in the first decade of the nineteenth century when the family heaped dirt and stomped it flat over the dead body of Jonas Shepard. Nine years later, Jonas was joined by his wife Esther, the old buried couple in each other's arms, at long last free from harm, the two spending their earthy days and nights dreaming the forest landscape.

Although I cannot say for sure, the fact that Mrs. Shepard and Mrs. Hill share the given name Esther seems to be more than mere happenstance. I wonder whether Esther, the wife of Samuel Hill, is the rightful daughter of Esther Shepard. I like to think she is. Their age disparity makes this possible, because the mother Esther would have been 39 years old when she birthed her daughter Esther. Somehow this tie-in makes the graveyard whole, as a family bloodline infuses purity into the boneyard's underworld.

The brief history of this burial ground is not done. There are expressive stories escaping the ground. Trusting the whispers of headstones, I sense clean-cut tales without beginning or end, accounts about the topspin of Earth beneath the glow of the sky, the tilt of the watershed unburdened of Pleistocene ice, the human affection for the greening of topsoil, and as Erazim Kohak so elegantly put it, "an acknowledgment of the truth, goodness, and unity of all beings, simply because they are, as they are, each in his own way."

The forest shines its ageless essence through all of us, and thus creates a vibrant community, its living members – all of them whether they are blackberries, woodpeckers, coyotes or people – harvested as tinder for fresh beginnings. The ecological traces are all around us. They are in the zigzag flit of fireflies, the wrinkled bark of trees, and in the golden shimmer of hayfields. It is these very kith-and-kin alliances that bind my fate to the corpses in this Brookfield graveyard, to the sumptuous biology of this place that is my adopted home where I will someday die.

The muddy pathways that slash the cemetery's myrtle point to habitual visits by locals like myself whose hearts absorb the shadowy incantations of these inhumed dwellers. Some callers bear gifts for their deep-felt presence. A few visitors have placed flowerpots, one plastic and one ceramic, at the base of Jonas Shepard's headstone to commemorate, I presume, the memory of the old patriarch long rooted to this spot of ground. The ceramic holder contains the dried-out stem and dusty leaves of an unrecognizable flower; the soil in the other supports a small American flag, a paper bar code curiously still affixed to the red and white stripes of its faded cloth. These simple human gestures provide ease of sort for us, the living, who come together with the dead, though far apart, to share the lonely, future prospect of daily life continuing without us.

Actually, believing that humans are mere unattached hulks, lunging out into earthly space with circumscribed lifetimes cut out of eternity by birth and death, simply cannot be. Rather, we are stonecrops, for every atom of our body derives its pith from the granite bedrock of Earth, the splendor of our nucleated cells emerging out of billions of years of unforeseen evolutionary spunk. Besides, we Earth-bound primates like all living things have nowhere else to go but back into the ground, to be swallowed into the belly of the predatory Earth, not as dead things but as ecological stirrings that inflame the soil. Each of our lives passes by and once over, there's more, much more than we realize.

The Brookfield boneyard extols the wild creations of death, as the merciless afterlife of flesh and bone dug into its underside is stood up on end as timbered ground, a family of corpses aged to soil and resurrected as majestic hardwood trees. Thick, weather-beaten butts of maple, cherry, and elm, none more than a century old, have sprung to life out of the graveyard's sod, mating the soil and water of the ground to the sun and clouds of the sky. Their ropy roots ramify themselves endlessly into the underground wilderness, searching the dark soil for humus-rich corpses encased in plank wood coffins. Over time, the root hairs and their fungal mesh, drinking hard and long from the rancid flesh, have drawn off the bodies into themselves, sending them upward into sapwood and leafing them out into the loose weather of the sky-lit world.

And so Brookfield's Shepards, Hills, and Hammonds still today have rhythmic lives of need and motion, if one imagines them spirited into the skin of woodland trees. From time to time in the low light of evening, I overhear their nineteenth-century murmurs echoing the forest breeze. For me, there's reassurance in these ecological contingencies, in the nonhuman forces of inevitability, a truth like that as firmly grounded in eternity as the solid Precambrian bedrock of Earth.

The story, of course, does not end there. Otherwise, there would be leanness in the early hours of the morning and in the idle moments of a nuthatch roosting on a branch of a rain-soaked hemlock. As dependable as the finality of our lives, each year the closed-in hazy skies of summer get washed out clean by the cobalt blues of autumn. It is then that the boneyard's hardwood leaves flame up fiery red and yellow before they let go and flit down to the woodland's floor. Scattered about the slippery mud, the now twice-dead specks of Polly Hammond and her Baby Jane rotted free from the grimy leaves and in the early spring blossomed out into the blueness of myrtle flowers and into the stink of skunkweed cloaking the nearby creek banks. Sooner than later and in roundabout ways, flecks of Jonas and Esther Shepard got digested and exhaled as the daytime chatter of squirrels and the nighttime screech of owls. Yes, like everything alive, we are fated to die unfinished and then forever to become.

THE TREE OF LIFE

"Trees….survive on a single breath per day. When the sun rises, they drink in a long, luxurious draft of its rays, and when it sets, they exhale a great stream (of gas)."

Han Kang, 2016. *Human Acts.*

I've spent much of my adult life in the pureness of forested landscapes. Long strolls through woodlands grown thick and full make me wonder about many things, both big and small. Forest thinking unties my crowded thoughts, letting the swell of this green sea wash over me.

Beneath the thick silence of a forest canopy, granite boulders, broken and stained, are strewn about in glacial till. Everywhere the sweet roots of maples and hemlock cling tightly to the shale ledge of a cliff side that is cracking apart by frost heaves. Fallen trees damp with moss quietly rot, spilling blood on the soil. A bad smell escapes the carcass of a partly eaten fawn, so small, lying half in and half out of the gurgling water of a creek bed. Nothing seems clear and clean as before. Discovery here is deep and unbroken. Air, water, rocks, and trees – the brashness of an undivided whole with endless time and meaning.

I've spent hours sitting beneath a river birch by a marshy pond littered with fallen leaves, and brooded. What are these things we call trees that rise out of deep, black dirt? In the way that reading mindfully goes beyond simply resting your eyes on words, seeking the quintessence of trees requires much more than looking at them with eyes. Actually what cannot be seen is what makes trees splendid, even wondrous.

Trees come in all sizes and shapes, the pint-sized ones being more shrublike than treelike, the big bruisers skyscraping upward into the open sky. Some trees sprout branches willy-nilly like the clutter of a woman's pincushion, whereas a circlet of twiglets crowns others. And in between, there's everything imaginable, as trees gussy themselves up with individual exaggerations and adornments. Consider velvety smooth barkskin, the kind that caresses the hand like the "glue and lime of love." However, the easygoing covering doesn't hold a candle to bark that is crinkled into side-by-side creases that look like, even smell like, the earthy furrows of recently plowed soil.

When we visualize trees simply as trees, we forget that all their treeness — every part of them — emerged from seeds that can be held in the palm of one's hand. Yet somehow, the genetic logic encapsulated in those sleepy seeds magically transforms them into lush woodland. Impossible to imagine really, but it happens wherever land luxuriates beneath the cool splendor of a forest canopy. Holding a handful of seeds is cradling a forest not just waiting to be, but wanting to be. This is the spunk of life.

Now, consider the sturdy massiveness of any tree. There's scarcely softness anywhere in its body. Trees are not just taut, but rock hard. Woodcutters are always honing the teeth of their saws, which dull quickly as they gnash and grind the spunky grit of even so-called softwood. But how in the world does a tidbit of seed grow tree matter and then stiffen it into a giant bole with its chapped burls and its out-of-line patterns of branches?

Well, biologists have learned that the chemical makeup of trees is unpretentious, consisting largely of carbon, hydrogen, and oxygen configured into an elaborate assortment of organic molecules. Also, they know well that order exists everywhere beneath the surface of things. The germination of seeds and the formation of heartwood and sapwood are all about DNA templates, cell division and differentiation, and countless, complex biochemical reactions that somehow set down firm, crispy wood tissue, molecule by molecule, layer by layer, year after year. Now, where does all that solid stuff that gets slapped together into a tree come from?

Anyone will tell you that trees are plants and plants grow from the soil. And because trees grow skyward, the obvious place to look for their wellspring is downward into the ground. There cloaked in the dark, mildewed dampness of this netherworld are gnarly roots and flimsy rootlets, all intertwined with purpose like the grimy limbs of mud wrestlers. A mish-mash of fungal filaments overspreads the tangled root mat, and together in this dank, chummy blackness they engage in revelry, feeding earnestly and drinking deeply from the bounty of the topsoil. It's a consumptive feast that kick starts the plumbing inside the tree. Once it's perking, the tree's robust juices are tugged upward through the intricate byways of its vascular system and stream even to the remotest prongs of its canopy.

But there's a paradox here, a transgression of physical law. As trees push their way upward and expand their girth, they transfer weighty mass – tons of stuff in the case of old-growth strappers – from the soil to their frame. Shouldn't this cause the surrounding ground to collapse into a huge crater? With all those massive trees feeding and growing, forest floors should be pockmarked everywhere with craters like the backside of the moon. And they're not, of course, as a jaunt along any forest trail confirms.

Well, it turns out that the explanation is as plain as day. Trees need water and they drink lots of it. Their thirst is quenched by slurping that "noblest of the elements" – H_2O – out of the soil. The rootlets draw the precious liquid inside of them and send it up to the tree's crown in exchange for food.

True enough, but where exactly does the water in the ground come from? From the air, of course, every time it rains. Water vapor high above the ground liquefies into mist, which swells into nimbus clouds. Obliged to run with the wind, these gray, lumbering clouds with swollen bellies sweat from the exertion and water droplets fall to the ground. The soils absorb greedily, the rootlets drink deeply, and the trees grow mightily.

So, there you have it, the fulfillment of a lifetime. The elements of hydrogen and oxygen – the solid building units of sapwood, heartwood, roots, bark, leaves, and seeds – ultimately are derived from the hydrogen dioxide gas in the atmosphere and only immediately from the dampness of the soil. Water vapor wafted by breezes, what we don't see, is transmuted into liquid rain and then toughened into sturdy forest wood. Gas to liquid to solid, a first-class triumph by any account.

What about the carbon locked in the tree? Like the hydrogen and oxygen, it's derived from the air as well. Leaves grab onto molecules of carbon dioxide suspended in the heavens and, at once, dull elements are transformed into gleaming gold. The dead molecules of carbon dioxide are given life by a tree.

Now you understand why gods must reign from the "roof of the world." By this life-giving deed, spiritless gases are animated into plant life and, when humans eat salads, into brainpower and thoughts. Implausibly, the solid, massive hugeness of a 120-meter-high sequoia is created out of nothing but invisible air. And as the tree soars splendidly upward, the ground remains far below, stable and stoic in its geologic demeanor, content with providing a fitting anchorage for such a majestic presence.

EDGE EFFECTS

"Death is alive, they whispered. Death lives inside life, as bones dance within the body. Yesterday is within today. Yesterday never dies."

Luis Alberto Urrea, 2005, *The Hummingbird's Daughter*, Back Bay Books, NY

Some hundred kilometers south of Sydney, a vast sky hugs a small coastal embayment chiseled out of basalt. Here, the Tasman Sea grips the craggy shoulder of Kiama. At my back are hills overgrown by a rainforest, at my front is basalt ledge awash in seawater. I'm standing on a point at the edge of southeastern Australia, a transmarine boundary represented by a bold ink line on coastal maps. Here the sea is stitched to the continent along a contour with zero elevation, a topographic datum between the upswing of the land and the downswing of the sea. Everything seems beautiful despite the tepid glint of a midwinter dawn. I sit still as stone, my thoughts entangled with raw emotion.

In the day's first light, the water appears heavy and frenzied. Disquieting melodies drain out of the sky. I don't hear as much as feel the wailing of wind and the thumping of breakers. There is no pretense whatsoever. The point of this violence is to put a goodly kink into the zero-elevation contour, so that maps of Kiama will have to be redrawn. The audacity of such tight-fisted purpose is the stuff of spectacle. Judging from the collection of passer-bys who linger nearby, I am not mistaken.

At last, dawn breaks. I stand atop the shore's stonework in wan light, and stare out at the sweep of ocean beyond the inlet. Steep, brazen waves with crested plumes of water are set to do harm, as they flit about offshore.

Having dropped its covering of whitecaps at low tide during the night, the sea is now poised to rise up and unleash its fury at the basalt cliffs. The rock-faces at the cove's head are tense, but sharp-witted, well aware that they must repel yet another onslaught by an infantry regiment conscripted by the Tasman Sea.

The shore is littered with the wreckage of bygone skirmishes – rubble heaps of shingle, messy landslide deposits, and threadbare, wave-cut cliffs. The forward lines of the basalt breastwork are battle-weary, their dirty, rusty rock faces lined with fractures and bruised from previous onslaughts by angry seas. Suspended low above the horizon, nothing more than a smudge, is the moon's fullness, which barely drops light onto the sea. Its inconspicuousness belies a looming influence on the day's events, as the spring flood tide, aroused by the enchanting sorcery of Luna, prepares to lift columns of combers and convey them to the disputed boundary line that separates the land from the sea.

The nervous fidgeting is about done. An army of strong-willed breakers, buoyed by rising tidewaters, advances shoreward. The day's onslaught of the land's fringe begins.

Wave crests, endless numbers of them, move forward, not as a gang of loutish hooligans, but as a legion of disciplined warriors. The wind exhorts its encouragement, and drenches the air with blood-curdling cries. The tactic is quite ordinary, a frontal assault of the basalt's embankment. The wave trains closest to shore advance at a practiced pace while maintaining a strict spacing between columns, a mathematical elegance necessitated by the friction of the shallow sea bottom.

The heaving combers, once in waist-deep water, get thrown off balance by the roughness of the cove's underside. Here, they get bad-tempered, as they stumble over underwater ledge and get twisted out of alignment. Some rash combers arc themselves into unbalanced curls and lurch forward, foolishly wasting energy. In no time at all, the battle lines devolve into patterns of confused, lopsided mounds of water unlike the gracefully aligned wave crests still approaching from offshore.

Moments before reaching the enemy battlement, hissing waves gather themselves into massive mounds of spilling water, twisting and weaving, as they leap forward with all of their might, slamming hard against the basalt. Tons of sea-green water explode against the pitch-dark stone. The air glistens with water droplets that mingle with the foul breath of ripped-up seaweed, rotting on the cove's shingle beaches. The sodden air, smelling of death, mutes the thumps of the crashing breakers, sounds that are more like distant mortar fire than the face-to-face onrush that it is.

The ground shudders with the seismic blows of plunging breakers. What damages the rock is not the water's impact as much as the force of the compressed air trapped in the fractured basalt. Limpid molecules of gas, squeezed tightly by the pounding water, strive to burst open the stones' interiors. The notion of water and air fissuring solid bedrock is counterintuitive and absolutely marvelous. But that's not all. The back-and-forth swash of the surf rolls debris about every which way. This surging water with its bedload of leaping sand and pebbles slowly grinds away the shoreline's roughness, burnishing its wave-cut platform to a glowing shine — beauty paradoxically fashioned by brute force. This is classic trench warfare, a conflict of slow, methodical wearing away of the enemy's resolve.

Like the flooding of tidewater, the faint ochre light of morning spreads out into the cove and shadows the irregularities of the land. Meanwhile, the moon, no longer visible, attends to time. The moments are self-absorbed with purpose – the breakdown of ledge by thoughtless acts of head bashing, a raucous barroom brawl of hooligans rather than the reasoned strategy of armies battling on a chessboard.

Despair hangs oppressively in the air. The world, it seems, has gone mad, bent on breaking down the land's steadfastness. Even passing children grow quiet and instinctively clutch an arm of a parent as they stare wide-eyed at the violent pandemonium before them. But splendor is splattered all over the rocky seascape as well, like the fractal drips of a Pollack painting. Breakers crashing against rocky shelves sprout sprays of water, alive with purpose. At every moment, hundreds of small and large spouts of water shoot upward into the sky in explosive glee and then rain down in silence, having lived momentary lives of poetic splendor. In death, they carry on in memory as foamy splotches that stain the gray-green skin of the sea. Along the cove's diagonals, huge breakers splash watertight rock, their splatter pooling and then tumbling off the ink-black basalt as miniature, lacy-white waterfalls. The cold emptiness of the morning air is now filled with textures and colors that grow, shrink, and vanish with the push-and-pull of the angry surf.

The black basalts of Kiama have fluid markings as well, mostly hidden from view. Their angular faces are etched with fine crow's-feet, weathered patterns that bespeak of a long-ago age. Now cold and stoic, wrinkled and cracked, the layers of basalt recall a time when each escaped individually as a lava flow fleeing from a magma chamber impounded in the darkness of the crust. Once free and uncramped, the fiery-red lavas seeped out of the ground into the glorious sunshine and puddled into fitting rock, forming stacks of basalt flows that now underpin Kiama's shore cliffs. Here they have long resisted the incessant attempts of storm waves to broach their stonework. This long-standing narrative of water and lava brimming over the land's edge is an heroic epic that predates Homer's *Odyssey* by hundreds of millions of years.

Reading and comprehending the complexity of the morning's noisy mayhem require heedful eyes and a dreamy imagination, coupled to a double-jointed mind. I've learned that it's best to step back and wait patiently, and things, even blurry things, sooner or later reveal themselves for what they are. And so today, I linger in anticipation.

Three young, clean-shaven men, clasping bibles and lunch bags, sit themselves at a picnic table near Kiama's inlet and proceed in no particular order to read, talk, eat, write, and think, ever aware and respectful of the consternation in front of them. The wind whips at their notebook pages. Shore birds, mostly white gulls with red-orange, stick legs, bicker raucously for food scraps fed them by one of the Christian men.

The treetops behind me dance about like drunken revelers as blasts of wind strip them of leaves and branches. A youngster on the far corner of the cove picks up an angular stone and tosses it clumsily into the surf, a pure geologic offering. Appreciative, the sea reciprocates and hurls rounded gravel and tattered seaweed onto the nearby walkway.

Curious drivers steer their cars to the southern shoulder of a nearby headland and from high up glare through windshields at the bedlam below, their idling engines spewing out noxious clouds of fumes that get swallowed up by wind gusts. For a few minutes, an old man blares his car horn as each surging breaker smashes the cliff.

On the upper strand, a bespectacled youngster with wet, dripping hair erases the salt crust that built up on his eyeglasses with a damp shirttail. His dog, old and slow, shoves her nose into a messy heap of flotsam dumped on a rock shelf and barks out wildness into the sky. Two plastic IGA-supermarket bags pulsate like tattooed jellyfish, keeping company as they warily circle the eye of a water eddy trapped in a far corner of the cove.

And the cross-boundary couplings between marine and nonmarine, whether robust or fragile, direct or roundabout, intimate or open, uninterrupted or sporadic, go on as they always have and always will. I am somehow reassured by the nature of these enduring tie-ups that today are spattered everywhere about Kiama's shoreline.

By late afternoon, the tide, perched high, pauses to rub sore muscles. The morning's labor of lifting up legions of combers against the down pull of gravity has sapped its energy. Thankfully, the long day is waning. The inlet is overflowing with glittering billows of white water overfilled with the foamy spume of breakers. Incoming swell now pass undisturbed far above the sunken rock ledge, and manage to get a purchase high on the shore's slippery basalt face before breaking apart. Still, the ardor and fierceness of the day have slipped away, faded out of existence, as has the moon.

There's more hissing than thunder in the cove now. Everything – sounds, motions, colors, textures, and patterns – seems more whispered than shouted. Because of the high-standing water in the cove, many waves reach the cliffs intact and then reflect off rather than break against rock faces. This causes them to crisscross and turn back on the still advancing columns of incoming waves. It's been a hard slog and everyone is bone-weary tired, ready to call it quits. And like them, I withdraw from a boundary that is neither land nor sea.

As I walk slowly uphill along the worn edge of the road, the day's revelry fills my mind. What exactly was accomplished today? Nothing really. Despite the daylong struggle, the land's boundary rock remained unmoved. Yet, even if the cove looked the same, it did not feel the same. I pause at the border of my landlord's property and turn to view Kiama's sea cliffs, a tilted wall of stalwart basalts. The flaxen sun is leaving quietly beyond the faraway rim of the world.

Even I am edged, I think. A fleshy membrane splits my-self from my non-self – me and not me. It's not that clear-cut though. Where exactly do I begin and end, as I breathe in and out, speak and hear, eat and drink, void and perspire, sense the warmth of another's body? The perimeter of my physical being, like Kiama's border with the sea, is blurred and does not end at my skin line.

While the late evening darkens, I lie quietly in bed, kept awake by my overactive mind. How discomforting to us modern humans is the overarching sweep of the deep past, which extends back to the very beginning of everything. Instead of facing this abstruseness honestly, we look the other way and then claim that the clock and the nanosecond are absolutes with metaphysical meaning.

I've noticed of late that many of my lived days and weeks are so interchangeable that I cannot tell them apart. Such similitude is self-serving, because it detracts from the realization that my bones and mind are sliding slowly and unwaveringly to the edge of my existence, to an eternal oblivion. The erosion of youth creates a lifetime of small memories, effected by incremental, moment-by-moment slips that for me have measured out into the bald-headed, bespectacled, gray-bearded man that I have become. When time settles, imagine what can come to pass at a shoreline laid open for millions of years to the sea's seething anger at being walled in by land.

Granted, today there was more cursing than biting at the seashore, more pain really than injury. The basalt cliffs of Kiama did not landslide into the surf. In fact, they were hardly nicked despite the frenzied extortions of the Tasman Sea. But I remind myself that today I appear to be no different than yesterday, except that I am one day older and so one day closer to my life's edge.

THE RANDOMNESS OF TRUE HARMONY

"Nature was not "a grave," "a kind parent," "a merciless stepmother." It didn't "abhor a vacuum," or "the old." Alas, it didn't abhor anything at all. It just went on perfectly. If nature was a story, it was a new kind of story; plotless, endless, at once both circular and linear, so vast it seemed not to move at all – a millennium hand, an eon hand – yet everywhere seething with a strange and wondrous energy..."

Nick Slouka, 2010, "Ecologue," in *Essays from the Nick of Time: Reflections and Refutations*

Murray Bail's *Eucalyptus* is a fresh, poetic novel, a sparingly written story of courtship set on an outback plantation located somewhere west of Sydney, Australia. It's an entrancing account of a widowed father with an "instinct for completeness, classification, order." He's obsessed with two yearnings: growing every known species of eucalyptus tree on his vast property, and ensuring that his daughter is married to "a golden-haired boy out of the ordinary...someone like your old father here..." The two desires are entwined. He demands that any prospective son-in-law must win the hand of his daughter by correctly identifying the hundreds of species of eucalypts that flourish on his estate.

The organizing principle for *Eucalyptus* is revealed at the outset of the novel as "the randomness of true harmony, demonstrated so casually in nature." The author's imaginings, engagingly quirky in themselves, are infused into the novel by the skillful usage of what at first appears to be a fortuitous assortment of tales about eccentrics in faraway places.

We are told hard-luck stories about a hunchbacked fruitologist in Carlton, Italy; a shoemaker in the Leichthardt suburbs of Sydney; three holy men from the Valley-of-Saints, Lebanon; a White Russian and a Latvian living on a dirt road south of Darwin; two Aussie soldiers adventuring in the Middle East; the Catholic Kearney living in Lifford, Ireland; Reverend Clarence Brown and his wife enduring heat and drought in Lagos, West Africa; and more than a dozen other allegorical narratives. These accounts are intermingled with refreshing musings about landscapes, art, beauty, and history.

And then, of course, there are the eucalypts. A different species of gum tree, every one of them associated with a tale or two, provides the heading for each of the novel's thirty-nine, short chapters. The sparkle and the energy that drive this multifarious saga forward to an unanticipated conclusion depend on the brilliance of a deft storyteller, one able to convey meaning and develop plot abstrusely. In effect, Murray Bail, like the imaginary father in the novel who personally collected and planted every known type of gum tree on his land, many more than five hundred species, has achieved in prose "the randomness of true harmony, demonstrated so casually in nature."

But what, you may wonder, does "the randomness of true harmony" mean exactly. After all, the essential qualities of randomness and harmony are at odds with one another, the former denoting a pattern that is not regular or uniform, the latter referring to a situation in which there is pleasing agreement. Rarely does anyone perceive ambiguity to be an agreeable state of being. Moreover, using the adjective true to qualify the condition of harmony implies that there is an absolute state of natural symmetry.

It seems to me that the gist of the phrase's significance lies simply in a loose rather than exact interpretation of the wording. And it's best to begin exploring the significance of this idiomatic expression by examining where, according to Bail, it is "demonstrated so casually in nature." Only then will we be able to appreciate the striking import of *Eucalyptus* as a distinctive literary creation of modern times patterned after the unpretentious wildness of ecosystems.

Natural landscapes are unevenly covered with assemblages of microbes, plants and animals. The resident organisms, like the resident characters of a novel, interact in simple and complex ways, not only with one another, but also with the bedrock, soil, water, and climate of their habitat. Such back-and-forth interactions between the living and inanimate elements of a region define the local ecosystem and its distinguishing set of biogeochemical processes.

Certain environments are stark and cold, others lush and hot, and still others are a mixture of these polar extremes. However, regardless of their specific ecological attributes, ecosystems have biographies filled with countless intertwined events, many resulting from happenstance. These "life histories" are uniquely the ecosystem's own in the same way that each of our ancestral and personal histories are uniquely our own. Portraying the natural world as an historical figure, it seems to me, is a clever way to conceptualize and thereby understand the diversified and far-reaching particulars of Earth's biological systems and their supporting landscapes.

Ecological existence, whether it is an individual life form, a community of species, or an entire ecosystem, emerges from a long-standing background of co-evolution. Imbedded in that legacy is a strong tendency for the biological communities to self-organize into quasi-stable systems that generally change slowly but inexorably over geologic time. If that were not the case, ecosystems and their ensemble of communities would be unsteady and so totter into messy disarray. If communities remain internally concordant, then their interdependencies serve to shore up the functions of the ecosystem.

Is the tendency for natural systems to self-organize the source of "the randomness of true harmony" that Bail allegedly uses to structure his novel *Eucalyptus*? If it is, can we legitimately equate his novel *Eucalyptus* to an ecosystem, and thereby compare its assemblage of interlaced tales to the patchwork of biotic communities that comprises ecosystems? Before we can properly assess these possibilities, a crucial distinction must be made between two of the key intellectual constructs of ecology – the ecosystem and the community.

Biologists define and delineate ecosystems functionally. A rainforest works in a particular way that is conspicuously different from the ecological functioning of a desert. What matters utmost in this conceptualization are the functional attributes of the system. By this I mean simply that the biotic components of an ecosystem are subsumed by the whole. In other words, an ecosystem's way of functioning, being largely independent of its specific biologic makeup, is self-supporting. It matters little what the exact plant and animal composition of a rainforest is, provided that it continues to operate as a rainforest.

By contrast, biologists define communities historically rather than functionally. This means that the integrity of a community depends directly on the particular membership of its species with their specific evolutionary and ecological legacies. Displacement or extermination of a key member species can have dire consequences for the community's integrity, and so the community whole is subordinated by the makeup of its species.

Given the legitimacy of these distinctions, where exactly is the location of Murray Bail's harmony that is "demonstrated so casually in nature?" At the scale of an ecosystem, the harmony is tied to its function, regardless of its specific ecological structures. In order for a rainforest to persist over geologic time, its various constituent communities, whatever the complexity of their organic parts and interactions, must operate in a particular way that is harmonious with the ecological functioning of a rainforest.

The species of flora and fauna that compose the tropical rainforests of Brazil, Australia, and Laos are distinctive from one another; yet each system functions as a tropical rainforest, despite their singular biological groupings. Therefore, it appears that the tenacity of any ecosystem depends on the congruent relationships of its constituent communities, whatever they are. In turn, this implies that the fortuitous, unplanned mosaic of communities that comprise a region's rainforest is a measure of its "true harmony," which allows the ecosystem to function both spatially and temporally as a rainforest.

The "true harmony" is imbedded in nature at the ecosystem level, and the "randomness of true harmony" in the chance historical particularities of each of the ecosystem's diverse webs of communities. And this, it seems to me, is where the ecological notion of "the randomness of true harmony, demonstrated so casually in nature" is starkly evident in Bail's novel.

The novel *Eucalyptus* can be likened to an ecosystem, and its miscellany of stories to an ecosystem's assortment of interlinked communities. The many vignettes of the novel, each offering individual characters with striking experiences, are interlaced life stories, in much the same way that an ecosystem's communities are particular entanglements of life forms with distinctive biological and evolutionary histories. Ecological associations emerge from nonlinear interactions and rarely are the result of the cleancut upshot of cause and effect. Instead, their complex organization reflects the strong sway of historical contingencies and the many interwoven, back-and-forth, chaotic processes that operate across a wide range of spatial and temporal scales.

Bail's use of narration likewise is roundabout and oblique, and although the tales appear sequentially on the pages of the novel, they do not proceed in a linear, step-by-step fashion to the storyline's final outcome. Individual tales cohere and make sense, though their tie-ins to one another and to the novel's plot are perplexingly obscure and seemingly random, similar to the working interactions of the sundry parts of ecosystems. Yet somehow, the dynamic and aesthetic qualities of *Eucalyptus* magically emerge, perhaps even self-organize, out of the novel's complex abstruseness.

In some ways, Bail's meandering style of narration and use of an obscure assortment of tales are comparable to the indirect, higher-order connections of biological systems whose self-organizing qualities have been identified though are not well understood by ecologists. By this account, Murray Bail has created a freshly imaginative work of fiction, a veritable representation of the "randomness of true harmony, demonstrated so casually in nature."

My point is that reading *Eucalyptus* is aesthetically and intellectually rewarding because of the novel's mysterious, multi-layered undertones of meaning that are patterned after the ecological workings of the natural world. The prose, structural style, metaphors, and allusions in Bail's novel profoundly enchant in the manner that the tangled harmony and spellbinding beauty of a rainforest's dense canopy and understory enthrall, even bewitch. Most importantly, the book's cryptic fables assembled by Blair accommodate and support the functional integrity of the novel in much the same way that the parts of a rainforest, its raveled latticework of biological communities and ecological processes, bolster its function. And so, Bail's protagonist, the father, creates an entrancing, harmonious landscape of gum trees on his estate, using a design template. This, it seems to me, is the essence of momentous creation, whether natural or artificial.

The creative approach used by Murray Bail to write *Eucalyptus* is an uncommon one in the human-built world. But rummage about long enough and you'll uncover examples of it here and there.

For example, I recall one cool evening at the On-Side Jazz Café in Sydney when two musicians, who had met one another just an hour before performing, agreed on impulse to jam together — the two of them alone without accompaniment. Earlier that evening, the proprietor of the On-Side Jazz Cafe introduced a middle-aged Dane, a sax player from Copenhagen and leader of an accomplished quartet currently in the midst of a six-month-long tour of Japan, Australia, and New Zealand. A locally, well-known, elderly pianist, an Australian friend of the owner and patron of the club, was the other member of the impromptu duo.

The initial onstage banter between the two musicians was awkward, even feigned, as both contemplated the dead of night found just beyond the familiar edge of day. Taut nerves jolted the thick silence of the club. The two, fidgeting about in a cramped space, quipped and chortled. Jittery fingers gamboled over burnished instruments. Odd chords and riffs collided head on in the still air. Although spontaneity and spur-of-the-moment improvisations were once the hallmark of jazz musicians, nowadays they seem to be exceptional occurrences.

This was genuine risk taking. They knew it and we, the audience, knew it. The duo was about to hurl itself into untrammeled musical territory, not creating in the engineered hideout of the studio or the reassuring privacy of a backroom, but brazenly in the harsh limelight of public spectacle. There was no turning back that night. Whatever was about to happen would happen to us all. It could be ugly and forgivable or pedestrian and inexcusable. Then again, it could be winsome and never forgotten. And just perhaps, the extemporaneous music about to be created could be especially fertile and visionary, a moment of serendipitous achievement when being alive becomes an extraordinary privilege.

Few artisans dare venture into this no-man's land of impulsive creation, although many allege that they have. This complex, unplumbed visionary realm, explored so expressively by Pablo Picasso, John Coltrane, and Jackson Pollock, is where creators strive not merely to render beauty, but to improvise it. The possibility that the jazz duo about to perform on stage could extemporize at a level of musicality commensurate with such ideals seemed exceedingly low, judging from their preliminary musical bandying and the fact that they had never before played together. They were venturing into unformed territory. No studio contrivances or safety nets anywhere, but simply two earnest musicians hoping to transcend their individual being and reveal something deeply beautiful about the human soul.

The young sax player deferred to the elder pianist, who selected a tune and began to play. And then it started, an attempt at spontaneous creation in a public venue by a chance meeting of musicians in a remote corner of a large city at the edge of Australia where the hot land tumbles into the cold sea.

Crisp bars, plinked from the keyboard, spread outward and upward, and took out-and-out charge of the club's silent interior. The Dane – head cocked, eyes barely closed, long muscular body pliant and swaying, left foot drumming the smooth-worn floorboards – listened from just off-center stage, holding his tenor sax loosely. Soon, he began to finger silent notes on his sax that only he could hear. Occasionally, his lips moistened the coal-black mouthpiece extending from the switchback turns of his brassy horn. Perspiration already beaded his broad brow, those dewdrops frozen in place by the blueness of an overhead floodlight. A shaft of red lamplight at the far left corner of the tiny stage burnt up the hot ivory keys of the piano. And there sat a thin, bald-headed Aussie in black vest and checkerboard sleeves, with shoulders, arms, hands, and fingers shaking loose a bluesy tune.

It may have been happening then, I suspect, a state of true harmony by the chance collaboration of these two musicians. All of it created by an audible pianist and a mute sax player. Only the Dane, improvising notes in his mind, could know for sure. Then again, the pianist may have sensed the Dane's silent notes in his soul as well. His fingers wailed joyously and he seemed entranced by all the playing jumping out of the two of them. The rest of us could only dream up what that intermingled sound might be. Whatever we imagined, I feel certain that it fell far short of their private, ad-lib composition.

After some time, no more than a handful of minutes, the soundless saxophonist roused himself. Even the blue wash of his face could not hide his bewilderment, even embarrassment about his private moments of soundless playing. Eyes now wide open, mind and body stiffened with apprehension, he leapt aggressively, though clumsily, into the mellow refrains of the pianist, but had to back out time and time again. His strapping notes, tentative and meddlesome, and far too complex, grated roughly against the smooth, bluesy flow of the piano. When given space to solo, he fell through the backdoor of the arrangement. The two of them, reeling forwards and backwards, finally ended the piece, obviously relieved to be untangled from that washout. Risk taking, I've learned, is mainly about failure. It must be why most of us avoid it at all costs and end up living such ordinary lives.

The second refrain of the set, a speedy bebop tune, began. This time, the sax was featured. The pair of them played back-and-forth, interchanging well-worn licks, as they worked around and through the complex harmonies, chords, and fast tempo of the hefty tune. It was nothing exceptional, simply first-rate jazz.

After about five minutes or so, the two hit their stride and stretched out. Then all at once, it happened. The saxophonist, emboldened by the tantalizing chord progressions of the pianist, slid into the beauty of an unforeseen, twisty logic. The pianist molded himself to the slipstream and followed along effortlessly. And then the two of them emerged on the far side of the glass mirror. Suddenly, everyone's fingers and feet were tapping and thumping, the bits and pieces self-organizing into a fervent whole, listeners pressing for more, the two musicians divining sharp interplay everywhere, all of it spiraling upward feverishly. Then, without warning, it was over, the glowing hot brilliance of the audacious moments extinguished forever except in memory. Thirty-two bars of unanticipated rapture, the fortuitous upshot of true harmony.

Live, unrecorded music is peculiar that way, in that it disappears at the very moment it is created. A faint trace of it exists only in memory recall. Such is not the circumstance for other art forms; novels, poetry, sculpture, and paintings survive well past their moments of inception.

Some Aboriginal rock paintings all over northern Australia, for example, have been around for thousands of years sheltered from the bleaching sun and caustic rain in caves or under rock overhangs. A rich assortment of these remarkable creations is tucked away in the crevices of a prominent sandstone escarpment at the "Top End" of Australia, the

Northern Territory's Kakadu National Park. The magnificent paintings themselves are naturalistic representations of a complex ecology of the imagination, motifs of large animals such as kangaroos and wallabies, fish, birds, lizards, turtles, crocodiles, humans, and powerful Spirit Beings, all of them depicted exquisitely on the smooth walls and ceilings of sacred rock shelters.

The art pieces are rendered in earthy pigments, primarily reds, browns, yellows, and whites, which are applied to the smoothly worn surfaces of burnished sandstones. Several painting styles are evident at Kakadu. One consists of stylistic stick figures, representing animated humans who are walking, dancing, hunting, or fighting. Another employs an "x-ray" style of painting, whereby the internal organs and skeletal framework are depicted as crosshatched lines within an animal's body outline. Fish, such as the perch and barramundi, are fittingly portrayed in this way, magically swimming about in the shadowy interior of rock shelters.

Stenciled impressions of human hands are also prevalent at many sites, individuals inscribing a living signature on the rock for posterity. Such hand stencils record the presence of people who were born, drew breath, had profound thoughts, and then died near that rock cliff that slices apart the northern Australia landscape. And thousands of years later, humans are able to sense their soulful murmurings.

Some of the more majestic paintings in Kakadu National Park, as well as elsewhere in Arnhem Land, are bigger-than-life depictions of ancestor Spirit Beings. Represented as either stick figures or x-ray motifs, their large male genitalia indicate their importance and power in the spirit world.

One of these beings, Namarrkon, the Lightning Spirit, is depicted boldly on some sheltered rock surfaces of the region. Two thick curved lines that look like an insect's feelers surround the Lightning Spirit's body, connecting his head, arms, legs, and testicles, a clear sign of Namarrkon's great physical and sexual vigor. During the monsoon season, which begins in November, furious cloud bursts of rainfall rage through the area. It is then that the Lightning Spirit leaps from the stone onto the menacing storm clouds that build up, where he growls thunderously and hurls lightning bolts across the dark gray sky. From high above the ground, Namarkon sees everyone, including those who have violated "The Law." As punishment, he pulls out a stone axe from his knee or elbow and throws it hard at the wrongdoer. Rarely does he miss.

All well and good, you say. These are certainly intriguing stories and relate to the transforming forcefulness of art, but what exactly is your point? Curiously, the walls and ceilings of certain sacred Aboriginal sites are overspread with paintings, veritable galleries of artwork. Commonly, the images are of widely different ages, with the more recent renderings layered over parts of the older ones in much the same way that younger sedimentary beds are superimposed on older sequences of rock, preserving their relative ages.

At first glance, the assortment of images in these galleries, the ancient ones likely thousands of years old, seems jumbled and discordant, with far too many incoherent paintings of fishes, turtles, wallabies, humans, and Spirit Beings, scattered about haphazardly in no discernible orientation. This perception is mistaken, however, in the same way that many Westerners misperceive the entangled wildness of natural landscapes to be messy and primitive, and altogether empty of harmony and meaning. Understanding the power of Aboriginal art, like the wild workings of an ecosystem, is making sense of a complex scripture that has a long-standing history of elaborate, self-organized evolvement.

The Aboriginal art at these sacred sites derives its mystical potency from the constituted artwork and the eroded physical space in the rock that together engender an organic whole. The natural pigments used to paint the images and the weathered stains of the sandstones diffuse into the glow of the indirect light that fills the sheltered space, which changes with the passage of the days' and the seasons' weather. Sometimes there is an austere silence near and far, and at other times a shrieking wind; both are an expression of an unseen, but deep-felt preternatural presence. There are no disjunctions here. What is there is a fervent sensibility of "true harmony" that allows the commanding mythologies of former times to enter the mind, spirit, and body of succeeding generations. The moment is never excluded from the past, nor the past from the here and now. The paintings on the smooth stone reinforce the relatedness of landforms, plants, animals, Ancestral Beings, and humans, imbedding them all in a unified eternity.

Apprehending the essence of rock paintings at sacred sites requires listening, sensing, and respecting the sanctity of the life-giving Earth, a force that embraces the soul of all existence. A rock, a mountain, a lake, or swamp may represent the body or trace of an Ancestral Being, the local Aboriginal people conceived by these powerful Spirit Beings. A human does not stand alone, but is part of an ongoing cosmic undertow, the cyclical renewal of incorporeal existence that has endured since the beginning of time. There is no parting of the ways between humans and Earth, but an intimate entwining of both into a spiritual, moral, and ecological existence.

The artwork at these sacred sites, painted over thousands of years by generations of Aboriginal people, conveys an unassailable truth about the created world. It is the realization that simple yet profound harmony pervades and unifies all existence now and forever.

As was the case for the musical duo's thirty-two bars of pre-eminent jazz improvisation, Aboriginal expression of this visionary state of the world through rock art was sought, but was largely unplanned. Rather, the collage of paintings at each sacred site slowly emerged from the overlaid vision of many generations of artists who painted images on the stone over millennia. The actual connections among the assorted images on a wall or ceiling may be unclear. Yet, the ensemble is an aesthetic whole, in the same way that the many stories in Bail's exceptional novel *Eucalyptus* cohere despite the first impression of their imprecise couplings.

No single Aboriginal individual knew what the final outcome of the artwork would be or would look like. It is the brainchild of fortuitous, shared self-creation across the generations, bit by tiny bit, in the very same way that the emergent complexities of ecosystems are the result of self-organization, chaos, contingencies, and co-evolution. By any account, these rock paintings are exceptional representations of "the randomness of true harmony, demonstrated so casually in nature."

It is through the deep philosophical and intellectual understructure of such ingenious creations of art, I believe, that demonstrate how intimately connected the humanities and the sciences are despite claims in academia to the contrary. Humanists and scientists alike derive inspiration from and their imaginations are set afire by the stark, impenetrable beauty of the natural world. This avowal needs elaboration.

Scientists endeavor to understand how the universe works and are now just beginning to grasp the far-reaching consequences of Nature's blind imagination. They've discovered that the exceptional biological diversity and beauty of Earth's wildness reflect complex co-evolutionary processes that paradoxically are inattentive, undirected, fortuitous, and inefficient. The structure, functioning, and richness of the planet's patchwork of ecosystems have emerged from a remarkable legacy of countless contingencies that occurred over billions of years of trial-and-error. Ever so slowly, an intrinsic ecological harmony emerged that scientists have intellectualized as theories of evolution, complexity, chaos, and self-organization.

Humanists are necessarily influenced by the scientists' revelations of Nature's fertile ways and some rely on such imaginative schemes to create exquisitely emotive art. As argued in this essay, "the randomness of true harmony, demonstrated so casually in nature" was used consciously by Murray Bail to organize his novel *Eucalyptus*, subconsciously by the jazz duo to improvise their thirty-two bar refrain, and consciously and subconsciously by generations of Aboriginal people of Arnhem Land and Kakadu to create their sacred rock paintings.

On the surface, this intellectual engagement seems to be a one-way interchange in that the findings of science impel the artistic achievements of humanists. More truly, it is a partnership, a two-way discourse of shared intellectual intensity, because scientists who internalize meaningful art, music, poetry, and literature rely on those revelations to scrutinize and think about the workings of the natural world. When one comprehends and appreciates the beauty, harmony, and organizational complexity expressed in art, literature, and music, one is inspired, indeed even compelled, to search for those very qualities in the cosmology, geology and biology of the world. This fanciful cross-pollination of both the fertile imagination and the lucid mind has set ablaze the visionary and aesthetic qualities of humanists and scientists alike, who are ever searching for "the randomness in true harmony demonstrated so casually in nature." How could the human world be otherwise?

MEMORY

"Every word is a category, a tool of abstraction, a criminal approximation. Every word removes the thing it is supposed to represent from the real world. Thus, every word is a lie."

Benjamin Hale, 2011, *The Evolution of Bruno Littlemore*

Words are complicated. They need to be, because they are the sinew that connects our embodied minds – our internal selves – to the exterior world. Languages enable us to think, speak, and write, and thus be human in a singularly evocative way. Yet, words, essential for recounting lived events and for retaining them in memory, are no more than an under-shadow of reality.

Do languages actually mirror the complex structures of the world? They do not, as any linguist will argue. If unconvinced, try to narrate the most fearful moment that you have ever lived. Or try describing the flood flow of a river when the entire riverbed is moving chaotically. The actual event, the personal experience of that actual event, and the narration of that personal experience of that actual event are significantly dissimilar. For example, the words "fear" and "happiness" are not the fear and happiness that we actually experience as whole-bodied animals. As such, the real world of lived happenings becomes whatever blurry stories we tell ourselves it is. And besides, as William Gass reminds out, "Words, so much more readily remembered, gradually replace our past with their own."

There is little doubt that without words, the species *Homo sapiens* would be intrinsically different than what it has become. In fact, Earth itself would be far removed from the place that it is today had words at long last not emerged out of the mouths of people. The lexicons of languages are so commanding that they have become geologic and evolutionary brokers in their own right. Entire forests have been razed, the chemistry of air, soil, and water has been altered, an accelerated extinction of species is underway, rivers have been obstructed and straightened, petroleum has been alchemized into plastic, and men have tramped on Luna's face, all of these achievements realized because of the transforming agency of human speech.

What is remarkable is not the scope as much as the rate of change that languages have unleashed in the world. Landscapes and climate are being transformed faster than ever before by the deft contortions of an astonishing muscle, the tongue, intentionally misshaped to create precise pulses of sound that are infused with human meaning and memory. The modulations of speech can induce delight, drudgery, dreams, despair, drama, distortion, dexterity, damnation, daring or whatever, all of these states attained by a tongue jigging and whirling molecules of air in a scrupulous manner.

Vibrations of air that sound out "Hey, you!" certainly have meaning, but do they have memory? After all, spoken words are merely lifeless pulses of sound, and memory requires some degree of sentience, does it not? An utterance, once free of the tongue, lacks any kind of comprehension, including a basic awareness of itself, and so cannot possibly have memory. But it does, of course, because the verbalization of "Hey, you!" into a sound pulse cannot carry that directive intact through air without it and so speech would be impossible.

The confusion arises from a misapprehension of memory's definition. Many equate memory with remembrance, even though the latter denotes the recall of information that is stored in memory and is not memory *per se*. Memory is about retaining information from the past. In its most basic form, it refers to the traces of preexisting occurrences, and exists independently of their recall. A sound pulse transcribed as "Hey, you!" has imbedded in its memory that first tickle of the speaker's tongue, as the wave disturbance spreads out into the air in all directions and causes someone's eardrum to pulsate to the refrain of "Hey, you!" The memory lodged in the sonic wave is the only anchor to what had just been shouted. Otherwise, "Hey, you!" becomes merely incoherent noise devoid of meaning.

Disavowing that a conscious mind is necessary for the retention of memory infuses all matter and all circumstances with vivid, earnest stories. For example, there's a huge fig tree growing in the Minnamurra Rainforest, which is located just west of Jamberoo in the Australian state of New South Wales. It has lived a long life – far more than five hundred years of wildness – rooted in the thin, but fertile, volcanic soil of a horseshoe-shaped valley that is carved into the prominent Illawarra escarpment.

What's impressive about this old timer is its immense girth, which is partially obscured by a skirt of busy epiphytes, a tattered cloth of twisted vines and clinging ferns. High above, the smooth bole grows a sun-drenched canopy of close-packed leaves that darkly shadows the forest floor. At first glance, it seems that all of the tree's mighty weight – its tons of sapwood and hardwood – is kept on end by the muscularity of a mass of entwined roots that reach down from high above and grip the ground tightly like the talons that they seem to be. In reality, the tree is a strangling fig, a parasitic plant that caused a hefty red cedar a slow death and a quick rot.

The tale of this die off begins simply. Long ago, a songbird trilling a tune defecated a small seed with its secretive genetic memory onto the broad elbow of a massive side-limb growing out of an ancient cedar. There it germinated in the thin, dusty soil that had built up quietly over the centuries. In no time the fig sapling – knee-high, green, and feisty – sent an aerial root from its perch to the ground far below and used this gangly appendage to quench its thirst and sate its hunger. Then magic happened. Ancillary rootlets, dozens of them, grew out of the parent root, grafted themselves to one another, and by degrees snaked themselves around the trunk of the cedar, coiling their way downward to root themselves in the forest floor. The red cedar, now tethered by the strangler's gnarly rootstock, some as thick as organ pipes, stood helpless and understated.

Legend has it that the red cedar soon was choked senseless, as the fig tree's roots in their own good time squeezed out the cedar's lifeblood like a boa constrictor cinching the breath out of a wombat. Death by strangulation, though, was not the cause of the cedar's death. In truth, the strangler tree's canopy simply overtopped the host's crown and blocked cut its light. Deprived of sunshine, the cedar leaves wilted, turned sickly yellow, let go, and fell to the ground.

Not much later, the dispirited red cedar, dehydrated and malnourished, gave up the ghost as well. Fungi and other decomposers feasted on the musty wood of the entombed tree, composting it in no time to sweet black humus. Ironically, even in death the cedar thrust up the fig tree, as its chemical disaggregates in the rich loam were sopped up by the strangler fig's rootlets and stiffened into spanking-new hardwood. There is justice in these ecological transactions, however, because the strangler will someday grow weary with age or succumb to disease, and be plundered by others as well, as life cycles into death and death into life in perpetuity.

The story is a gripping one. But did it really take place as told? Where exactly is the memory of that happening? After all, the red cedar was digested largely out of existence as if it never was. Actually, a trace of the cedar's life is safeguarded in the dark enclosure of the fig tree's entangled root mass, where it's preserved as vacant space. One can peer into the gaps between the corded roots and glance at the empty interior. The hushed shadows in the fig's root buttress are soaked with memory of the once-living tree that gave the huge vault its elbowroom. And this ghostly vestige, like the paper rubbing of a tombstone inscription, is a trace that persists in memory as negative space.

Yes, stories are wherever you care to look. The world, every part of it, teems with the memories of countless past occurrences, both small and large, both recent and ancient. Memories ensconced in inert matter like stones and landscapes can be given life when joined to the doodling imagination of a human mind.

At first, the remembrances of long-ago memories may be free-floating and seem baseless, and even be inconsistent with the recollections of others, a measure not of the failure of memory as much as of the fertility and uniqueness of each reflective mind. But if treated respectfully and given a fitting context, the accounts of past happenings, whether specific or general, lead to earnest stories, tales that are delightful for those people who care to understand them. The stories of Earth are all about beginnings and endings, including yours and mine as well as everything else that exists today whether inert or alive.

Consider a sequence of buff-colored sandstones stranded on a steep hillside bordering a paddock in the hilly countryside of southeastern Australia. Preserved in its physicality is a proud memory – the existence of a now-vanished inland sea. Familiar with the vernacular of sedimentary rocks, I interpret the sandstone's birthright by examining the size, shape, and arrangement of its grains, the rippled and cross-bedded adornments of its strata, and the ghostly forms of its trace fossils.

What is recalled is a circumstance far back in time when tides, waves, and currents colluded to arrange endless scores of quartz and feldspar grains into tidy blankets of sand that covered the shallow bottom of an inland sea. Once the sand deposits were built up, vagrant invertebrates homesteaded the seabed. Clams, worms, and shrimp excavated burrows in the soft sand and lived contented lives in relative peace and harmony in their sunless dwellings.

Tragically, none of their bodies were preserved after death. However, a ghost town, a profusion of burrow infillings engraved in the rock, provides memory of their way of life and testifies to the existence of a once-prosperous community of bottom residents. The architectural framework of the tubular dwellings in some cases is so distinctive that, remarkably, it's possible to identify the genealogy of the tenant, sort of like distinguishing the building styles of nineteenth century farm cottages of Ireland from those of Wales and Scotland.

The mute sandstones have a lot to say to whoever is attentive and learns to apprehend them. About midway up the section of rock, a crooked erosion surface slashes across the sandstones' flat bedding and lops off the roofs of burrows in what was once a crowded neighborhood of clams. A band of coarse gravel, as thick as a muscular man's arm, hugs the erosion surface and forms a tight-fitting seal over the unroofed dwellings of the bivalves.

The storyline is a familiar one. A violent storm, perhaps a hurricane, struck the bottom community of this shallow sea. The rise and fall of massive waves raised by gale-force winds tore up the backside of this flat seabed. Sand grains were ripped off the sea bottom and scattered every which way by strong, unruly currents. Layer after layer of fine sand was worn away and the burrows, all of them, were dug up.

Clams cowering alone in the dank cellars of their burrows were smothered, an outrageous ending to the great days living in placid, sun-drenched water. The storm finally broke. Mercifully, a layer of rough gravel was spread across the scoured ground, transforming the yard of dead things overnight into a burial ground. What is momentous about this particular saga though is that the memory of this storm is several hundred million years old! Think about it – a one-to-three-day-long happening recalled not just from the latter-day ages of the Pharaohs, but from the secretive memories of Earth's deep geologic past.

There is a pithy incident stored in the long-term memory of those silent rocks, a stone's throw from the bivalve graveyard. Here there are groupings of sandstone layers embossed with eye-catching cross-beds, so logical and sharp that they must have been chiseled out of the rock face by artisans. They weren't. These cryptic structures actually register the movement of water. Each is a still life of the world as it once was. In shallow seaways, bottom currents stirred the sand and whimsically shaped the grains into stunning bed forms, Lilliputian replicas of wind-formed dunes on land. Their profiles are lopsided in an agreeable way. The unbalanced shape captures tension, as flowing water rode roughshod over the seabed, and rolled sand granules up the gentle backside of sandbanks and pushed them over their crest. Shoved hard, the particles toppled down the front side of sea dunes and collected into thin beds that are as steep as loose sand can lie. These leeward laminations are the cross-beds of the sandstones that speak so eloquently about their watery origin.

There's even more to tell. Two distinct patterns are evident in the sandstones. Some layers have cross-beds tilted to one side, others lean in the opposite direction. What's noteworthy is that the two types alternate with one another up the entire rock section. They remind me of frames in a film clip of a tennis volley that show the heads of spectators hinging back-and-forth as they track the ball.

The bi-directional cross-beds indicate that the bottom currents had swung around, first streaming in one direction, then in the other, and then back around again, over and over. Such indecisiveness is a mannerism of tidal flow, especially near seashore inlets where tidewaters get pinched by a narrow channel. Here, the current is forced to reverse its flow with the passage of each flood and ebb tide. It's clear that the current was swift, because smashed bits of clamshells pepper the sand. Also, there's a shortage of burrows, suggesting that the sea bottom was made unstable by the fleet-footed current and was not suitable for permanent settlement by organisms.

The stark arrangement of the cross-beds enthralls. I approach the outcrop and isolate a couplet, a lower sandstone bed with cross-beds canted to my right and an upper set inclined to my left. Their combined thickness amounts to less than a third of a meter. Incredibly I realize that, like the wizardry of Einstein, I can transpose space and time. Assuming that the tides in this now-vanished sea were semidiurnal, the solid beds of rock transfigure into half of a solitary day in Earth's history that was lived several hundred million years ago. What's even more astonishing is that the sublime tidal work of a much younger moon than the one perched above me last night was literally cast into stone, encased in the still memory of this cross-bedded rock, and through the refractive imagination of a human, its voice was recalled back to life. If this had not come about, those moments of that half-day's surging tides would eventually have been obliterated forever.

Realizing this, I am reassured; time does carry the past into the future. A companion, exhilarated by this discovery, exclaims that knowing the thickness and the time it took for the couplet to accumulate makes it possible for me to calculate a sedimentation rate for twelve hours of that long-gone day. I don't. Somehow a bald-faced number diminishes the freshness of the sandstone's storyline about switchback tidal currents induced by a moon that was 200 million years younger than it is today.

Existence may be matter-of-fact, even foolish, but it's not half-witted. This is surely the case for the granules that I glimpse in these age-worn layers of stone. Granted, they are exiles, displaced from their home waters long ago and now forced to live on the far side of an Australian paddock. Nonetheless, like all things, they are multigenerational and so their narrative grows out of roots buried in the fertile soil of the past. Their memories, resplendent with color, texture, and poise, have backbone. The beds of rock are populated with countless grains of sand, every one of them an emigrant from some far-flung place of the world with a yarn or two to share with anyone who cares to listen.

The vast majority of the quartz grains are roughly hewed with the caustic, angular edges of peasant stock. There are so many and so ordinary that they all look alike. Their original home was a granite rock exposed at the base of a remote mountain ridge that, by the way, no longer exists, worn away to flatness forever by rain and river water. These broken granules arrived at the tidal inlet, exhausted and angry, mostly homesick for a hillside view of the sky, after having endured a rough-and-tumble journey to the sea as part of the river's coarse bed load. Once at the seashore, they suffered the humiliation of having to create a new life underwater.

Eventually their provincial doggedness paid off. The ocean, tired of their whining and fussing, abandoned these crude grains long ago. Now the seabed has hardened into the ledge of a hillside that curls around the brink of a farm pasture and forms the headwater for an unpretentious creek. The view is good and the air is fresh.

Residing among the peasantry are sophisticates. A headcount from one sandstone stratum revealed that they comprise a small share of a large community of quartz grains, much less than one percent. Their distinguishing features are ball-shaped bodies and sallow complexions. Unlike the roughened appearance of most of the others, these grains are as smooth and as well rounded as Nature allows, a few in silhouette approaching the flawlessness of an Aristotelian sphere. On top of that, an exquisite pearly luster, as elegant as the soft glow of the moon, dignifies their stately bearing. Spiteful neighbors, and there are many, whisper to anyone who will listen that this gleam of theirs is icy cold, nothing more really than a crust of hoary frost, and with this one remark dismiss their inherent beauty altogether.

If only they knew. The smooth luster, whether deemed pearly or frosty, turns out to be an affliction, a severe acne condition. Ironically, a profusion of tiny pits, thousands of them, scars the exterior of these near-perfect spheres of quartz. Fortunately for them, the pockmarks are microscopic and blur out into a satiny polish. In actuality, each pinprick is a memory of a single impact, a head-on collision with other granules as the wind tumbled these grains about.

They likely began life as ordinary angular bits of quartz that broke off a weathered slab of granite from somewhere unknown. Once free, the wind blew them away and, spirits high, the grains somersaulted gleefully over the ground. Each jarring bounce inscribed a tiny flaw onto their glassy surfaces, and bit-by-bit the quartz grains were worn smooth and pearly, the proverbial ugly duckling transformed into a comely swan. They lay at rest for a long while on the front side of a tall desert dune with a fine view, a strip of peach-colored beach that faded into a wash of cobalt-blue sea. One gray day, a biting offshore wind grabbed some of them and, in the blink of an eye, they were whisked into the chilly water of a nearby tidal inlet, where a rough-hewn peasantry of angular quartz grains, in great numbers, had already settled in.

Other breeds of quartz are scattered about the rock. To find them, one needs to visit specific addresses, because most inhabit a particular stratum of a high-rise, rock sequence. The effort to find them is well worth it though, as some have unheard-of tales about their former life and homeland.

Take the case of the "diamond-back" grains, a bunch of elitist particles found only in a single bed of the entire outcrop, specifically in a thin layer of sandy siltstone that is tinted sage-green and located far up the hillside near an old gum tree. Here, dispersed among the silt and sand grains, are found a few clean-cut crystals of quartz. In profile, they look like exquisitely-shaped diamonds, flattened a bit from top to bottom, and as translucent as the see-through water of a coral sea. Their corners are not pointed but rounded, softening what would have been a harsh outline.

The "diamond-backs" talk big and loud at the drop of a hat about a time long ago when they had been drifting aimlessly in a thick stew of magma, simmering deep inside a volcano. There in that subterranean caldron, they grew precise crystal facets by absorbing molecules of silicon and oxygen dissolved in the magma. Life was wholesome and good, and had meaning. It was about chemical law tempered by the pure and simple dance of atoms.

One day though, everything changed. The volcano's plumbing ceased up and the gas, which before had been bled out of the magma chamber more or less regularly, built up to unbearable pressure, until the throbbing force blew out an entire flange of the mountain. The blast was ear shattering; ash, blobs of lava, and pulverized rock were blasted skyward by the sonic explosions. The biggest projectiles fell rapidly around the outside perimeter of the gaping crater, the smaller rubble settling farther out on the lower volcanic slopes and the adjoining valley floor. The dust particles, mainly fine ash, were blown so high in the air that the uplift of the Trade Winds took hold and conveyed them to the periphery of the land. Most were blown out to sea, whereabouts unknown. The fortunate ones, like the "diamond-backs," dusted the seashore of an inland sea.

What's truly unbelievable is that some of the "diamond-backs" survived being blown up to smithereens completely unhurt, their flawless beauty unscathed. In trying to make sense of this, they proclaim to anybody who will listen, and especially to one another, that this unimaginable outcome was fated to happen and that they must be a 'chosen' variety of quartz. In all honesty though, only a few were left undamaged. Most were scarred, many disfigured horribly by the volcanic blast, their bodies now broken and twisted.

In any event, all of the "diamond-backs," whether whole or not, take pride in a bigheaded way that they got to the tidal inlet of an inland sea by sliding down clean slopes of air, rather than tumbling along the murky bottom of a river. This is the source of their haughtiness and the reason that the peasant masses mock them as "diamond-backs".

Earth loves to talk about herself. Her trees and rocks speak eloquently of their past. Many people would rather talk than listen, and mostly chatter about themselves and about others who matter to them. And this life habit, easily acquired, cultivates a self-centered perspective about existence and value. How could such an inward-directed focus not lead to self-seeking ideals? What's most disturbing is that it produces children, women, and men who are deaf to the poignant stories spoken by strangler fig trees, cross-bedded sandstones, and abraded quartz grains. And sadly, this impairment disallows any appreciation of the ripeness of their bloodline, which unfurls back into the deep past individual-by-individual, generation-by-generation, species-by-species to the earliest stirring on a lifeless Earth.

As most people imagine it, before them was dark time or no time at all. Looking fondly at their children and grandchildren, they feel blessed that the future will be glorious, the promise of a lifetime that is mostly about them alone. And, of course, the human spirit in order to flourish requires much more than the blandness of the self.

In spite of their assertion that intrinsic value is unique to the human race, some talkers do appreciate the outdoors. They love to linger in the warmth of the sunshine and to drive across pastoral countryside or through vast forests that swaddle spiny ridgelines and towering mountains. When they talk about such experiences, their comments invariably are about enjoyment, relaxation, contemplation, and beauty. It is clear that a strong utilitarian vision frames their understanding of, and hence interaction with, the natural world. Put simply: if I like it and can use it, it has value; otherwise it doesn't.

Meaning and worth in such an obdurate mindset are derived exclusively from utility, and "wild" landscapes are significant merely as an untapped resource for human gratification and recreation. Regrettably, this uncompromising way of imagining the wildness of the world interferes with learning anything from the ungraspable, ancient memories inscribed deep inside their bodies as DNA molecules as well as in the stones of the natural landscapes around them.

I recall a day in the Minnamurra Rainforest of southeast Australia encountering people who were enraptured by the green lushness that overfilled the rock shoulders of a small ravine. An unbounded history was being felt by a few of us who were lingering in the wet silence of the space. Implausibly, a "Permian day" had reemerged. Cool dampness, burbling water, mossy boulders, soggy snags with fungal threads, ferns lingering in dank shadows, creepers gripping hulking trees, slippery clouds of leaves everywhere above.

Without warning, the dreamy moment was shattered. Two gleeful children being chased by a knuckle-walking father howling like a chimpanzee, rushed into the day, all of them caught up in mirthful play. They hardly paused, disappearing as quickly as they appeared, memory of their father's grunts and their collective laughter lingering like a pungent smell. They were having fun as a family, entertaining themselves in the rainforest in the only way they knew and, by doing so, were oblivious to the affecting, sublime stories all around them.

The modern world is generous with its material wealth for those who can afford it. But there is a tradeoff – a demanding life of stressful work that, as the rhetoric of advertising assures us, will create personal affluence and provide life fulfillment. And so, each hour of our controlled days is filled to overflowing with responsible busyness and business, whether we relax or toil. And this manner of living habituates the mind to the maxim that "time is money." Not wanting to squander our monetary moments on Earth, we fill our leisure time with resolute activity and the natural world is then construed as a mere diversionary backdrop for earnest recreation.

With such a perspective, people are disinclined to spend 'wasteful' hours listening quietly to the unspoken language of a rainforest. And so a family cavorts through the Minnamurra Rainforest as a clan of noisy chimps. After all, what else is there to do in a wilderness that is devoid of organized entertainment except to fill the quiet stillness with loud merriment?

This peculiar way of living – the ultra-consumerist's way of life – is a cultural conferral that has prevailed largely in the West for no more than a century or two. Now, capitalism has been globalized. This lifestyle is a guise that has been daubed over the memory of our inborn instincts and natural feelings. Notwithstanding our urbane manners, what our animal species is about and what is encoded in our genes are the long-lived memories of a hunter-gatherer being living in the wilderness before it was deemed a tangled wasteland.

How else to explain what happens to even the staunchest materialist who spends time out of hearing of his celluloid life, roughing it in the backwoods of a mountain landscape? Gradually, this overworked, distraught, human creature slows down and listens to the primal stirrings of stones, trees, and sky. Slowly, biological time disarranges the minutes and hours of the clock. It is then that a powerful sense of something more exalted, more hallowed, than the human circumstance emerges, and the sun suddenly dawns as never before. There are no words, just the push-and-pull of primordial memories deep inside his body. Something primal unlatches as his DNA molecules whisper their speechless story to a human temporarily prepared to listen to himself become deeply alive. Without warning, his internal ghost-man rises and spins a whirlwind dance of bliss. Grateful to recall what real living is about, he stares at himself in euphoric disbelief. And then he heads back home!

A NATURAL HISTORY OF THE SOUL

"The beautiful spring came; and when Nature resumes her loveliness, the human soul is apt to revive also."

Harriet Ann Jacobs, 1861, *Incidents in the Life of a Slave Girl*

Throughout history, people have striven to overcome the fearsome, biological finitude of human life. For many, this requires a muscular belief in an ethereal soul. By claiming that souls are deathless, people willfully transcend mortality and become grander than ordinary animals.

This claim, of course, conflicts with the weight of evolutionary history and is at odds with the primordial rawness of Earth, a place that is unencumbered by purpose and goal and is overfilled with inefficiency, carelessness, and contingency. And yet Earth throbs with the explosive splendor of mountains, granites, pebbles, bacteria, fungi, millipedes, aspens, voles, wolverines, grizzlies, and humans, churned together by relentless sunshine, moon glow, rainfall, and wind flow. If you squint at the thick of it, the pieces come together whole and yet are mostly loose from one another.

On any given day, the world and its parts undergo changes that are mostly as slow as soil creep, peppered occasionally by avalanches, volcanic eruptions, and earthquakes. Nature is not concerned with well being, whether it's the graceful geometry of a sand dune with a long view of the seashore, a clutch of mountain poplars leafing out along a floodplain, or jazz riffs swirling about the sweaty air of New Orleans. Over the course of deep time, change and adjustment are unending. In actual fact, Nature has no authenticity, and simply becomes whatever it comes to be, a process of incessant improvisation, of ever-flickering stirrings without endings. Nature, in effect, has a heart of stone.

Renouncing the truth of the world as perceived by science, insisting that its discoveries are unjustifiable and atheistic, disavows the absolute nature of our human origins. Whatever we claim to be must grow out of our animalism, bestowed to us by the natural world. From this planet-bound circumstance, the notion of an ethereal soul, taking "wing" from Earth upon the death of the body, trivializes the deeply sublime, grimy roots of our humanity.

The underbelly of human life is layered thick with metaphysical significance. Take the human soul. If it exists, the soul like the body was born of stones and soil on the globed Earth, our only home. We cannot ever truly understand ourselves until we glimpse the rock shadows of our soul's natural history. From the ground and its bits of clay mixed with carbon, nitrogen and water, and pierced by roots and clutched by fungi, came up the fierce consciousness of human existence. As Dorian Sagan explains in *Notes from the Holocene*, "unfeeling particles …. (gave) rise to feeling beings." That is the beguiling truth of our genesis, our emergence out of Earth as an embodied animal entangled in a web of diverse life and so, like everything else, ripe for eventual oblivion.

All long thoughts about sand dunes, poplar trees, and jazz tunes are infinite, because as the novelist David Brooks exclaims in *The Fern Tattoo*, "… everything connects to everything else and that no story can exist if one doesn't learn to wrench it free…" The philosopher and novelist Michael Frayn enlarges this point. He writes in *The Human Touch*: "But there are histories out there waiting to be recorded!…No, there aren't… There is the *evidence* from which histories can be written, once you've decided what's relevant to a particular interest. Until then there's just a great undifferentiated, overlapping tangle, without sense or even sequence, waiting for someone to discover a few loose ends and pull out a few usable threads, then to weave them together into a usable fabric."

A sea of evidence indicates that today's life forms co-evolved blindly by random mutations and natural selection. These processes in tandem created species while stuffing the graveyards of slate-gray cliffs with the fossilized relics of extinct life forms. Looking backwards, stratigraphic intervals of siltstone, shale, and volcanic ash speak plainly about the heaving out of *Homo sapiens* from beneath the leaf shade of a Pleistocene sky.

Stone memories abound, and are filled with innumerable objects and processes strung together in deep-seated darkness – a slantwise vanishing point that leads back into the faraway past with its unfamiliar geographies. What's clear is that Earth since the advent of geologic time has been obsessed with oblivion, with the forced departure of long-forgotten seaways and ridgelines, with the recurring mass extinctions of species and their ecological webs. Imagine the prodigious graveyard that absorbed 3.8 billion years of dying so that the natural order of today could leap into life. Consider the unbounded heaps of death ahead of the 21st century, as fresh grasslands and estuaries, unsullied rainforests and coral reefs, pristine ocean trenches and alpine peaks, spill out of the unformed deep future into the now and as quickly slide away forever into the geologic past.

All species, ecosystems, and landscapes are fated to vanish, each and every moment abandoned to the past. Otherwise, there would be no room for the new days of new life. As quipped by E. M. Cioran in *A Short History of Decay*, "The human adventure will certainly come to an end, which we may conceive without being its contemporary." This underworld of decay, death, and extinction that buttresses the fresh beauty of each of our lived moments is the only way Earth can be, meaning that all things "…to be submitted/ To the tingling dance of atoms once again," as noted by the Poet Laureate Robert Hass.

The fact of this fact is profound. The grace of our human lives emerged, astonishingly without volition and consciousness, from the ruination of all things that existed before us. Denying this fact of science misrepresents the thud of reality, the springboard for all earthly existence, together with the creation of heartfelt human emotions despite the weighty indifference of Earth.

Yet, notwithstanding the findings of geology and evolutionary biology, simplistic accounts abound about the long history that led to the 21st century world. What's deeply troubling is that most people believe that the evolutionary genealogy of *Homo sapiens*, no matter how natural, is harsh and even shameful, and so cannot be true.

But stones don't lie, people do. All that we are or ever can be is a stunning terrestrial animal, set free to ponder good and evil, and to think, feel, and speak of things both real and imagined, both true and false. Once the fleshy mind of humans acquired sense knowledge, a species for the first time ever on Earth distinguished a past from memory and a future from imagination. As E. M. Cioran bemoans, "I was, I am, or I shall be – a question of grammar and not of existence."

Despite our ways of abstraction and rationalization, notwithstanding our superegos and illusions, at the day's end we are wholly embodied and finally will die, each of us, despite a stubborn, faith-based belief that humans are extraordinary beings unlike anything else on Earth. Ernest Becker in *The Denial of Death* writes: "This is the terror: to have emerged from nothing, to have a name, consciousness of self, deep inner feelings, an excruciating inner yearning for life and self expression---and with all this yet to die."

The contrast between what our human nature is and what it ought to be is jarring. We are mortals and should be talking about it, for it seems far better to reflect on the mud soiling our body than to stumble upon it unprepared at the end of one's life. This is the splendor and horror of the human condition, the empty depth of human power and thoughts to conciliate the world to our immortal wishes.

The reality of finite existence, of humans fated to be expelled from life, seemingly demeans human self-esteem, dumping us empty-handed into death and then back to stone. The naturalistic account of *Homo sapiens* forces upon us the cruelest torment possible, the existential audacity of a "de-souled" being who must endure a brief, indecent life of ongoing decay, finalized by death into nothingness.

If we renounce a human soul, many people believe that they will become unhinged and go mad, given the inherent pointlessness of finite human existence. But is that necessarily true? Why does the soul need divine inspiration, given that our species evolved by natural selection? Why can't the human soul find deep roots in the biology of the body, the ecology of Earth, and the enormity of deep time? What is the connection between self and corpse? Cannot the natural grounding of the human soul in the Earth's humus provide affirmation of the self without resorting to supernatural agencies and false promises? Can true meaning ever emerge on Earth where stones are in charge, where nothing endures forever?

The basic question that needs to be addressed is: How possibly can an ethereal soul exist independent of a divine presence? In other words, can the soul be embodied in the flesh and blood of the human animal? And if so, what do we mean by a soul that is bounded by the physicality of the body?

One way of naturalizing the soul is to liken it to the 'self,' the unique attributes at the heart of our individual, singular lives. No two people have ever been alike, nor ever will be. We are born, we ripen, and we die, our bits remixed into the planet's humus. Without an immutable soul and an afterlife, the essence of human existence becomes the grace of the body. The splendors of our lived days emerge inwardly out of multiple forms of singularly embodied experiences, both conscious and unconscious, that are centered on thoughts, imaginings, emotions, feelings, patterns, events, and relationships. We survive, learn, and prosper and by so doing derive meaning from our interpersonal, environmental, and social stories.

In a meaningless world, a glorified existence relies on such experiences that are unique to every human who has existed, as well as those yet to be born. So the soul is not the body, nor is it the mind's consciousness, and, hence it is not a corporeal thing. I conjure the soul to be an emergent quality, a spillover of complex internal processes rather than a discrete entity. In this view, the soul cannot exist apart from the body. In essence, there is no ethereal soul except in our imagination.

Understood in this way, there is a natural history of the soul that emerged from the complexity of evolutionary processes. Being deeply social creatures, we internalize the experiential richness of our unique, daily lives. The singularity of every human's life – one's birth, one's surroundings, one's inner push-and-pull of age-old memories, and one's death – can be construed as an individual's soul.

Yes it is mortal, but paradoxically it is not, simply because we persist in the thickset, shared memories and stories of those who knew us and are still living. Once these people die, our soul vanishes and has become, in some sense, ethereal, unless your natural soul happens to be an exceptional one and is 'immortalized' as legend to be shared by humans not yet born.

CPSIA information can be obtained
at www.ICGtesting.com
Printed in the USA
LVHW041131050820
662441LV00006B/1618